A
Nation Under Siege

The Civil War in Wales 1642-48

Peter Gaunt

Cadw
WELSH
HISTORIC
MONUMENTS

LONDON: HMSO

FRONT COVER PHOTOGRAPHS:
A detail from Sir Anthony van Dyck's triple portrait of King Charles I, painted 1636-37 (Reproduced by gracious permission of Her Majesty the Queen).

Raglan Castle, home of the fabulously-wealthy marquis of Worcester, one of the king's principal supporters in Wales during the war.

'Roaring Meg', a mortar that may have been used during the siege of Raglan in 1646. It was designed to lob explosive shells on to a target.

INSIDE FRONT COVER:
Wales in 1610, from John Speed's The Theatre of the Empire of Great Britaine. *The map shows towns and larger villages, rivers and bridges, and some of the higher hills and mountains. The four cathedral cities of the country appear in the corners (By permission of the British Library).*

TITLE PAGE:
John Williams (1582-1650), exiled archbishop of York, returned to his native Conwy to defend castle and town for the king during the civil war. This engraving depicts Williams dressed as a 'musketeer', exchanging his mitre for a helmet. His weapon is shouldered, and in his left hand he also carries a matchcord, used to ignite the charge, and a musket-rest. From the bandoleer around the archbishop's shoulder hang small containers, each holding a charge of gunpowder, and a bag of musket balls. (By courtesy of the Ashmolean Museum, Oxford).

© Copyright — Cadw: Welsh Historic Monuments 1991

First Published 1991

ISBN 0 11 701222 X

Edited by David M. Robinson and Diane Williams

Designed by Tom Morgan

Maps and plans by Cartographic Services, Welsh Office

Typeset by Afal Typesetting

Printed in the United Kingdom for HMSO Dd 293651 5/91 C100

Oliver Cromwell (1599-1658) dressed in black armour, with his page tying his sash. Robert Walker's much-copied portrait was painted after the war in the late 1640s, when Cromwell was lieutenant-general of the parliamentary army (By courtesy of the National Portrait Gallery).

HMSO publications are available from:

HMSO Publications Centre
(Mail and telephone orders only)
PO Box 276, London, SW8 5DT
Telephone orders 071-873 9090
General enquiries 071-873 0011
(queuing system in operation for both numbers)

HMSO bookshops
49 High Holborn, London, WC1V 6HB
071-873 0011 (counter service only)
258 Broad Street, Birmingham, B1 2HE
021-643 3740
Southey House, 33 Wine Street, Bristol, BS1 2BQ
(0272) 264306
9-21 Princess Street, Manchester, M60 8AS
061-834 7201
80 Chichester Street, Belfast, BT1 4JY
(0232) 238451
71 Lothian Road, Edinburgh, EH3 9AZ
031-228 4181

HMSO Accredited Agents
(see Yellow Pages)

and through good booksellers

Sir Anthony van Dyck painted this triple portrait of King Charles I (1625-49) in 1636-37. It was intended to help the Italian sculptor Giovanni Bernini to execute a bust. When Bernini saw the painting, he is supposed to have said that the king appeared 'doomed . . .'. He went on: 'Never have I beheld features more unfortunate' (Reproduced by gracious permission of Her Majesty the Queen).

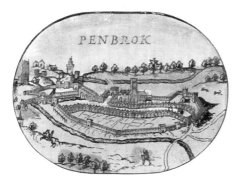

A sketch of Pembroke in the early seventeenth century by John Speed. As in the Middle Ages, it remained essentially a single street town, enclosed by walls and defended by its mighty castle (By permission of the British Library).

Contents

Introduction

Raglan Castle seems to encapsulate the history of the civil war in Wales. The seat of the most powerful royalist aristocrat within Wales, it was one of the first bases to be garrisoned for the king at the outbreak of the war, and it was the last principal mainland stronghold to fall to parliament at the conclusion. In the early days of the war, the prince of Wales was entertained here as he tried to raise men and money. And, in 1645, with the war all but lost, King Charles I stayed here for several weeks, mulling over past failures and future options. Throughout the civil war, Raglan was a centre for royalist operations over a wide area of south-east Wales, and it was a formidable obstacle to any parliamentarians hoping to break into the southern part of the country. In 1646 the castle endured a prolonged, formal siege and bombardment, which have left their mark not only on the masonry of the castle itself, but also in the weathered earthworks of the adjoining fields. The gaping great tower bears unmistakable witness to the deliberate slighting of the castle by parliament when the war was over.

Many other physical remains of the civil war survive in Wales, sometimes less obvious or picturesque than Raglan, but all important in retelling and illustrating the history of the conflict which engulfed the country during the 1640s. Well over thirty castles within Wales saw military action at some stage of the war, and a number of walled towns, great houses and churches, together with at least one former abbey, were caught up in the conflict. Bullet-marked walls, ruined castles, and a peppering of soldiers' graves, all bear witness to the civil war in Wales.

In this context, it is appropriate that Cadw: Welsh Historic Monuments should be concerned to produce such a volume in its series devoted to various themes and periods focusing upon the 'built heritage' of Wales. Cadw cares for, and directly administers, many of the properties mentioned within the text. The organization also has a general responsibility for all ancient and historic monuments throughout the Principality, and works to protect, preserve and promote them.

The principal thrust of the volume is the war itself, the major conflict fought between 1642 and 1646, and the rebellions of 1648. In order to place these military events in context, the book also looks at the background to the war years, at the situation in Wales in 1642 when war broke out, and, to some extent, at local government and administration during the period of conflict.

Contemporary quotations have usually been reproduced in their original form, complete with the variable spellings of this pre-dictionary age, though the text has occasionally been repunctuated for clarification. All dates are old style, but the year has been taken to begin on 1 January, and not — as was common practice at the time — 25 March.

A mighty fifteenth-century stronghold, Raglan Castle was transformed into a veritable palace during the Tudor period by William Somerset, third earl of Worcester. It was his grandson, Henry Somerset, created first marquis of Worcester in 1643, who held the castle for the king throughout the war. Following the capture of the castle in 1646, the royalist garrison was permitted to march away 'with Colours flying, Drums beating, Trumpet sounding'. The great keep (to the left of this view) was deliberately wrecked by the parliamentarians. One side of it was brought crashing down, either by explosives or by digging beneath the walls, temporarily supporting the masonry with timber props and then igniting them.

Wales at the Time of the Civil War

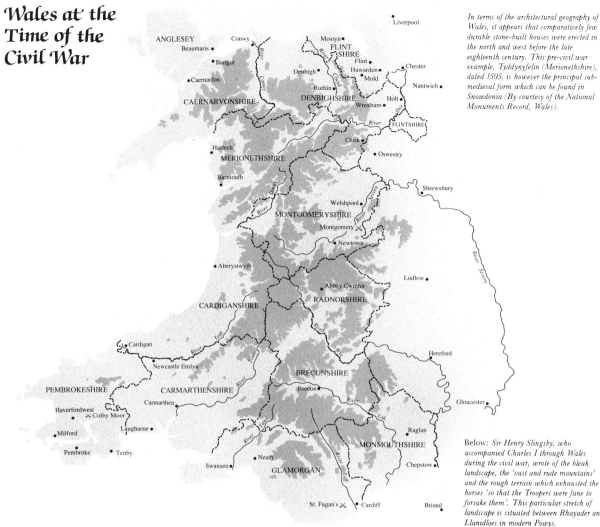

ANGLESEY
Conwy
Beaumaris
Bangor
Caernarfon
CAERNARVONSHIRE
Liverpool
Mostyn
FLINT SHIRE
Denbigh
Flint
Hawarden
Mold
Chester
Nantwich
Ruthin
DENBIGHSHIRE
Holt
Wrexham
FLINTSHIRE
River Conwy
River Clwyd
River Dee
Harlech
MERIONETHSHIRE
Chirk
Oswestry
Barmouth
River Dovey
Shrewsbury
Welshpool
MONTGOMERYSHIRE
River Severn
Montgomery
Newtown
Aberystwyth
Ludlow
Abbey Cwmhir
RADNORSHIRE
River Severn
CARDIGANSHIRE
River Teifi
Cardigan
Newcastle Emlyn
River Teifi
River Wye
Hereford
BRECONSHIRE
PEMBROKESHIRE
CARMARTHENSHIRE
Brecon
Gloucester
Haverfordwest
Colby Moor
Carmarthen
River Usk
Milford
Laugharne
Raglan
Pembroke
Tenby
MONMOUTHSHIRE
River Towy
Chepstow
Swansea
Neath
GLAMORGAN
River Taff
Bristol
St. Fagan's
Cardiff

In terms of the architectural geography of Wales, it appears that comparatively few durable stone-built houses were erected in the north and west before the late eighteenth century. This pre-civil war example, Tyddynyfelin (Merionethshire), dated 1595, is however the principal sub-medieval form which can be found in Snowdonia (By courtesy of the National Monuments Record, Wales).

Below: Sir Henry Slingsby, who accompanied Charles I through Wales during the civil war, wrote of the bleak landscape, the 'vast and rude mountains' and the rough terrain which exhausted the horses 'so that the Troopers were fane to forsake them'. This particular stretch of landscape is situated between Rhayader and Llanidloes in modern Powys.

Chapter 1

Wales on the Eve of War

There markets good, and victuals nothing deare,
Each place is filled with plenty all the yeare,
The ground mannurde the grain doth so encrease,
That thousands live in wealth and blessed peace.

The poet Thomas Churchyard, writing in the late sixteenth century, heaped lavish praise upon Wales and the Welsh. He found only beauty and abundance in the countryside, and such honesty and prosperity in the natives that a stranger could safely wander the land with 'purse of gold in hand, / Or mightie bagges of silver stuffed throwe'. Other contemporaries, particularly English and foreign travellers viewing with the jaundiced eyes of an outsider, saw a very different Wales, a Wales of poverty and backwardness, of mean-spirited, Welsh-gabbling farmers eking out undernourished livings from the sparse land. In the 1630s one estate on Anglesey was described somewhat unattractively as 'course and wilde grounds without hedges... not a stick of wood growing upon any of them nor any firing besides gorse and ferne, the houses... but cotes, not fitt for a civil man to rest himself in for an houre or two much lesse to lodge in; the tenants verye poore, living chiefly as most of the tenants of these parts do upon oate and barley bread and butter milke and whey, glastwr [skimmed milk] and such like trash'. Such were the conflicting descriptions of the land over which king and parliament fought in the 1640s.

In the eastern borderlands and in the Vale of Glamorgan there is a good deal of evidence for a significant amount of rebuilding in domestic architecture prior to the civil war. In Montgomeryshire and Monmouthshire, wood was often the material used. As at Tó-hesg (Llantwit Major), a long-house of about 1600, the Glamorgan examples are generally stone built (By courtesy of the National Monuments Record, Wales).

The Geography of Wales

Geography divides Wales into two parts. Almost two-thirds of the country comprises fairly barren uplands, 600 feet (180m) or more in height, ranging from hills and moorland to harsher beacons and mountains. The shortened growing season, the generally wet, cool, Welsh climate and often poor or shallow soils meant that in the seventeenth century this land was suitable for little more than fairly rough grazing and limited, subsistence cultivation. The uplands were thinly populated, dotted with isolated farmsteads and occasional hamlets, and crossed by few roads. When he marched with the king's army from Presteign to Newtown in September 1645, Richard Symonds noted that, 'except in the first three myle, wee saw never a house or church, over the mountaynes'. Nominally held by the king at the start of the civil war, and in due course falling to parliament, in practice these uplands largely escaped bloodshed and were not actively contested in the 1640s.

Instead, civil war generals sought to control or conquer the more prosperous and populous Welsh lowlands. In addition to the narrow plains of the north and west coasts, there were larger tracts of relatively fertile land in the south (the Vale of Glamorgan, parts of Gower and

The late medieval seal of Tenby emphasizes the town's role as an active port. In the seventeenth century it was one of several west Wales ports which maintained a generally buoyant trade with Bristol, the north coast of Devon and Cornwall, as well as parts of France. Other significant ports in the south-west included Cardigan, Carmarthen, Haverfordwest and Pembroke (By permission of the National Museum of Wales).

The market hall, built around 1600, in the small Montgomeryshire town of Llanidloes. Attracted by the surrounding cloth industry, the population of the town was growing in the seventeenth century. At the time of the war it may have been up to 800 (By courtesy of the National Monuments Record, Wales).

An illustration of cloth making in the seventeenth century. The cloth is being dyed and then stretched out to dry on tenters, held in place by tenterhooks.

most of Pembrokeshire), in the north-east (chiefly the Vale of Clwyd and Flintshire), and to the east along the Marches or borderlands with England. The rivers Wye, Severn and Dee and, to a lesser extent, the Usk, Towy, Teifi, Dovey and Clwyd, cut valley inroads into the central uplands. The valleys and rolling countryside provided not only reasonable pasture but also better soil for crops. In the seventeenth century, the majority of the population lived in the lowlands, and here were found all the important towns, ports and main roads of Stuart Wales. Men, money and tolerable communications made these areas tempting to king and parliament alike.

Following several decades of substantial growth, the combined population of Wales and Monmouthshire was probably approaching 400,000 in 1640. The overwhelmingly upland counties of Radnorshire and Merionethshire had the smallest populations, Glamorgan and Denbighshire the largest. On the eve of the civil war, barely 10 per cent of the population lived in towns, no Welsh town was large, even by contemporary standards, and in our eyes most would be dismissed as mere villages. Wrexham, with perhaps 2,500 souls, was the largest town in north Wales, Carmarthen the largest in the south. Few others had more than 1,500 — 2,000 inhabitants.

Despite the growth of the pre-war decades and the appearance of some extra-mural suburbs, the town plans which accompanied Speed's county maps emphasize the small and compact nature of seventeenth-century Welsh towns. Even town dwellers would have been physically very close to the fields and open countryside, and economically dependent upon them. For most seventeenth century Welsh men and women, the countryside provided both home and livelihood. Seventeenth-century Wales was overwhelmingly rural.

The Early Seventeenth-Century Economy

Stuart Wales was essentially pre-industrial and almost everyone made a living from the land, either directly, as farmers or agricultural labourers of some sort, or indirectly, as brewers, millers, dairy workers and others depending upon agricultural produce. In pastoral areas, cattle and sheep were the mainstay, while in mixed farming areas, considerable quantities of oats, wheat, barley and rye were grown as well. Apple and pear orchards were particularly common in Monmouthshire. The land could yield other harvests, though they played a secondary role at this time, exploited by large landowners merely to supplement their agricultural incomes. Thus woods and forests were felled for timber, stone and lime were quarried, some metals — chiefly lead and copper — were mined and smelted on a small scale, and coal was dug in the south and the north-east. Down to 1640 they were overshadowed by the long-established 'industries' based upon wool and hides — spinning, weaving, cloth-making, tanning and the manufacture of leather and leather goods.

Throughout the pre-war decades, the Welsh economy was heavily dependent upon trade. The quickest and cheapest way to move goods was by water. Wales was blessed with a long coastline containing many natural and man-made harbours and with a number of rivers navigable far upstream. Silting was already proving troublesome in several estuaries and the activities of Barbary pirates, operating all round the western coasts, caused further difficulties. None the less, the Welsh had a generally buoyant trade with Bristol, Chester and

Liverpool and, further afield, with Ireland and the Continent. Travel by land was much slower and more expensive, effectively precluding the large scale development of coal and metal mining inland. But some goods had to be moved by road, chiefly cattle driven on the hoof and cloth carried by convoys of pack horses. The Welsh economy depended upon this cattle trade — Archbishop Williams called it the 'Spanish fleet of North Wales which brings hither that little gold and silver we have' — and outlets into England were essential. Although cattle could be driven as far as London for sale, farmers and cloth workers alike depended upon vital markets in the Marches. Chester, Oswestry, Shrewsbury and Ludlow were outlets for produce from north and mid Wales, while the *entrepot* of Bristol sucked in most of the south Walian trade.

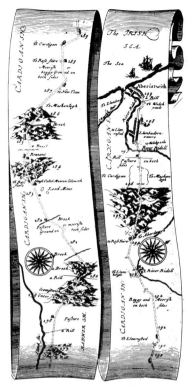

Right: *This detail of a 1675 'road map' of England and Wales is from John Ogilby's* Britannia. *It shows the last section of the road from London through mid Wales to Aberystwyth, a section which involved crossing both high hills and 'boggy and moorish' ground.*

Below: *John Speed's map of Caernarvonshire in the early seventeenth century. Speed was impressed with the 'craggy hills' which dominate the county and which he felt 'may not unfitly be termed the British Alps'.*

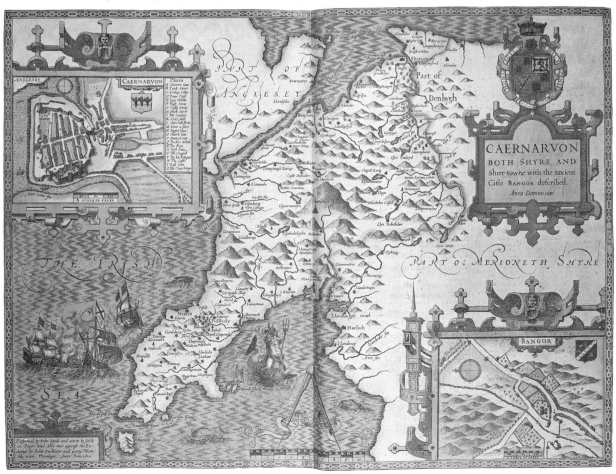

9

Castles at War I: Rebirth

The civil war became a protracted struggle to hold and conquer territory, to control towns, fertile lowlands, the main roads and ports. Military, administrative and financial control was exerted from a string of local strongpoints, usually containing a garrison, arms and ammunition. They also served as prisons, places of refuge for people and their possessions, and centres for defence or counter-attack. Although many types of buildings were caught up in the conflict, most Welsh strongpoints were located in the medieval castles strung around the coast, overlooking estuaries and river crossings, and guarding the borderlands. The civil war witnessed the rebirth of the Welsh castle, for more than thirty fortresses saw active service during the 1640s.

The civil war followed 150 years of relative peace, years during which medieval castles had become somewhat unnecessary and certainly unfashionable. A few royal castles, such as Chester and Ludlow in the Marches, had been carefully maintained for administrative purposes. There were others, perhaps a dozen or so, which remained the seats of noble families and had been kept in good repair. Indeed, several — Carew, Laugharne, Powis and Raglan, for example — were extended or remodelled during the sixteenth century to provide grander and more comfortable domestic accommodation. But most Welsh castles, royal and non-royal alike, had been virtually abandoned by the end of the fifteenth century, or were disgarrisoned and allowed to crumble during the sixteenth. When the antiquary John Leland toured Wales in the 1530s he found the great majority of medieval strongholds unoccupied and in poor condition. At Manorbier, for example, he found 'ruins', though 'many walls yet standing do openly appear'.

This was the state of many Welsh castles on the eve of the war. Some were so ruinous by the 1640s that they could play no role. A few more were in good condition. But many had been unoccupied for several decades and were in considerable disrepair, though not totally ruined. They were roofless shells, their interiors decayed or collapsed perhaps, but with sound and defensible outer walls. Once a castle fell into disuse, the roof quickly sprang leaks, water entered, and the roof timbers, main beams and floors would decay and eventually collapse. The mighty stone and mortar walls, however, were very durable and often survived almost unscathed. Such castles could be repaired and brought to life once again to meet the needs of war.

Repairs and extensions were hastily put in hand, to reroof and refloor the disused shells, to erect further accommodation for garrisons, arms and armour, to renew gates, to renovate and strengthen walls, and to insert gun platforms from which muskets and ordnance could be discharged. In many cases, additional defence was provided by digging earthworks beyond the outer walls, either encircling the entire castle, or covering specific weak points, particularly gateways or areas overlooked by high ground. Such earthworks could take the form of trenches and banks, and were sometimes strengthened with stone or timber. Smaller crescent or 'V'-shaped embankments or bank and ditch projections were also employed. The latter were often in the shape of arrow heads behind which ordnance could be deployed. Traces of such defensive earthworks survive at Raglan, Carew, Manorbier and elsewhere. The most advanced earthwork was the separate, earthen artillery point or 'sconce', almost a small fortress in its own right. One survives on slightly higher ground adjacent to the northern lake at Caerphilly Castle.

Although Caerphilly Castle played little part in the war, an earthen fort was built to defend the approaches. Here covered in bluebells, from the plan below it seems the earthwork comprised a rectangular platform with projecting bastions at two of the corners, upon which cannon would have been mounted. The central hollow was probably to protect ammunition or soldiers. A Roman fort lies beneath the much disturbed site.

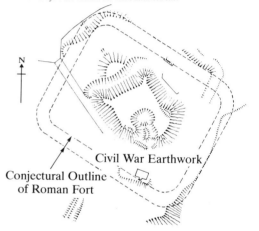

N

Civil War Earthwork

Conjectural Outline of Roman Fort

Although John Norden wrote in 1620 that Holt Castle was 'now in great decay', his accompanying drawing shows a well-preserved pentagonal stronghold. Both castle and adjacent bridge across the Dee were of key importance during the war (By permission of the British Library, Harley Ms. 3696, f. 5).

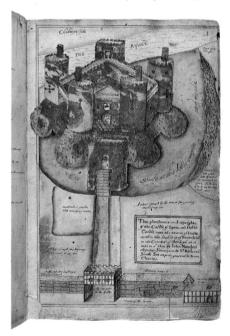

The north wing of Carew Castle was built by Sir John Perrot (d. 1592) during the latter half of the sixteenth century. The huge outer windows illustrate that defence was no longer paramount in 'castle' building. The upper floor contained a typical Elizabethan long gallery.

Powis Castle (above) and Chirk (below), as sketched by Thomas Dineley during the 1680s. Both castles had been well maintained and modernized during the century preceding the war, and both played major roles in the conflict (By permission of the National Museum of Wales).

A contemporary drawing of Conwy about 1600, at which time it was a small town with fields and undeveloped land remaining within the walls. The large house with formal gardens near the top is Plas Mawr, a superb Elizabethan mansion built in 1576-80. Although the borough was thriving, a survey of the castle taken in 1627 revealed decayed roofs and rotten, collapsing floors (By courtesy of the marquis of Salisbury).

Society in Stuart Wales

In an era of inflation, rising prices and falling wages, the majority of the population, urban or rural, probably saw their social and economic standing decline in the pre-war decades. A series of harvest failures during the 1620s and 1630s certainly produced widespread distress in Wales as in England. But the established elite weathered the storm, cementing their social superiority by exploiting their estates, enclosing land, bringing former commons and wastes into use and repeatedly raising rents. Although the Welsh elite may not have been as numerous or as wealthy as their English counterparts, most counties could boast an interlocking, intermarrying network of perhaps two or three dozen leading families. Territorial magnates, the great peers of the realm, were thin on the ground in Wales in the seventeenth century, and most counties were controlled by a block of gentry, leavened with the occasional second rate peer. The greater gentry had annual incomes of £500 or more and often held baronetcies or knighthoods; their lesser colleagues, worth perhaps £200 per year, would often merit the title 'esquire'. Bolstered by land, wealth and influence, a suitable coat of arms and an illustrious genealogy, real or invented, the greater and lesser gentry together monopolized county government and offices, and led both society and politics. The gentry dominated Stuart Wales and ran almost every aspect of life within the Principality.

The arms of John Blayney, carved in 1636, at Gregynog, Montgomeryshire. Blayney was a member of a long-established gentry family, many members of which fought for the king in the civil war. John himself was royalist high sheriff of the county in 1643. The devices seen on this panel are all armorial bearings of the ancient princes of Wales. The Blayneys, like all native Welsh gentry, claimed descent from one or more of these princes (Reproduced by permission of the Warden, Gregynog and the University of Wales Press).

Wales and King Charles I, 1625-39

Where the gentry's lead would take the Welsh in the event of civil war was not immediately clear. Wales was a distinct country, physically, linguistically and culturally separate from England. It was far away from London, and inevitably somewhat detached from the political developments and controversies of the capital. Moreover, news and views were invariably printed and transmitted in English, a language which the majority of Welsh men and women could neither read nor understand. The gentry were better informed, but they had generally benefited from royal rule in the century or so before the civil war, gaining property at the dissolution of the monasteries (1536-40) and power, status and money by holding offices under the crown. Thus a mixture of detachment from the political controversies of London, self interest and a general conservatism and innate loyalty ensured that many Welsh men and women felt strong ties of duty to their divinely appointed and anointed monarch. These ties were strengthened by deep and genuine fears of attack by hated Catholic powers, and an intense awareness of the vulnerability of the Welsh coast to invasion by the Irish or the Spanish. Accordingly, there was a tendency to rally round the crown in times of crisis and to give military or financial support as required.

King Charles I, painted by Daniel Mytens in 1631, soon after he had embarked upon his prolonged period of non-parliamentary rule (By courtesy of the National Portrait Gallery).

But this support was neither unquestioning nor unlimited. Heavy or repeated royal demands for men and money quickly strained the limited Welsh resources, particularly during the years of harvest failure and depression of the 1620s and 1630s. Contemporary records are littered with pleas of poverty and exhaustion and muffled rumblings of discontent. A few went further and criticized the drift of Charles I's policies as tending towards tyranny and the ruin of his people.

During the 1630s Charles ruled without parliament, relying instead upon non-parliamentary revenues, chiefly 'Ship Money', an ancient royal right to collect ships, or their cash equivalent, from towns and counties to defend the country in times of danger. For much of the 1630s Ship Money was levied annually in every county, with the Welsh counties and Monmouthshire together assessed at over £10,000 per year. In most years the bulk of the money came in, and several times the Privy Council thanked Welsh sheriffs for such prompt and full payment. Only at the very end of the 1630s did Welsh counties seriously default. Wales, after all, had much to gain from an expanded navy and strengthened coastal defences, the ostensible ends of Ship Money.

But there were complaints that the tax was reducing Welshmen to poverty and that its collection was an unpopular and divisive business. In 1637 the sheriff of Cardiganshire complained that 'endeavouring to levy the Ship Money, he tried by all fair and gentle means, but could not receive one penny, so that he was compelled to distrain oxen, kine, horses, sheep, household stuff and implements of husbandry, the which petitioner can get no money for, nor any man to offer for them one penny, though often set at sale'. A few Welshmen went further and voiced deeper objections, questioning the legality of Ship Money and linking attacks upon it with demands for another parliament.

At the same time Charles attempted to reform the church by placing greater stress on the role of the priest, introducing more elaborate services and rearranging and beautifying church interiors. During the 1630s three of the four Welsh bishoprics — St Davids, Llandaff and St Asaph — were in the hands of bishops who supported and implemented these policies. Attempts to overhaul the church, clergy and church buildings may have been both necessary and welcomed by some, and the return to more visually attractive, ceremonial forms of worship may have pleased many Welsh men and women, with lingering affection for the old religious ways and customs which had been undermined by the increasingly austere Church of England. The Reformation had been very slow to take hold in Wales, and an Elizabethan bishop of Bangor had written of the 'dreggs of superstition' he found among his flock, their veneration of saints, relics and holy images, their 'indecent vigils and... much pilgrimage goyng'. Charles's reforms of the 1630s might be in tune with such feelings.

Without parliament, King Charles was dependent upon non-parliamentary revenues, chiefly 'Ship Money' — an ancient royal right to collect ships or their cash equivalent from towns and counties. This illustration shows part of a document prepared by the sheriff of Caernarvonshire in 1637-38, recording the amount of Ship Money to be paid by each parish in the county (Copyright: Public Record Office, SP 16/380, no. 98).

William Laud, archbishop of Canterbury (1633-45), the architect of the king's ecclesiastical policy. The archbishop's 'Laudian' or 'Arminian' reforms of the church aroused great hostility in some quarters. This is a contemporary copy of a portrait by Sir Anthony van Dyck, dating from the mid 1630s (By courtesy of the National Portrait Gallery).

Although many existing churches were rearranged during the 1630s in line with Laudian reforms, very few churches and chapels were erected at this time. One such is Rug chapel, built by William Salesbury, later royalist commander and defender of Denbigh. Externally, Rug is a simple, rather plain rectangular building of grey stone.

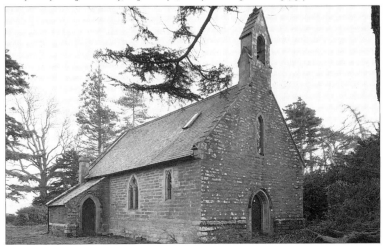

The plain exterior of Rug chapel contrasts sharply with its rich interior, complete with carved pew ends, a grand candelabrum, wall paintings, and an elaborately-carved roof. The cut-out wooden angel (above) is one of a set attached to the roof trusses; the carved panel (above right), with the strange beast at the centre, forms part of a frieze running around the base of the roof. It was precisely this sort of interior decoration which infuriated many low church Protestants.

Thomas Wentworth, earl of Strafford, painted by or after Sir Anthony van Dyck around 1633. Strafford spent much of the 1630s governing Ireland for the king. Recalled to England in 1640, he became a prime target for many MPs generally aggrieved at Charles's political, religious and financial policies. Strafford paid the price and was attainted and executed in spring 1641 (By courtesy of the National Portrait Gallery.)

Yet to others, Charles's religious policies appeared as attacks upon the true, simple Protestant faith of Elizabeth I and James I, moves to create a greater distance between men and their God and, worst of all, attempts to reintroduce Roman Catholicism by stealth. Stuart Wales was racked by anti-Catholicism, by fears of a Catholic invasion or home-grown uprising, and the king's religious policies locked into and heightened this outlook. In parts of Wales, particularly the larger towns, there emerged groups of outspoken critics of the Caroline church, vocal and vehement Protestants who could be labelled 'puritans'.

Breakdown and Crisis, 1639-41

In the late 1630s, religious disputes of a similar nature triggered off rebellion in Scotland. Once more, Wales rallied around the king, contributing 500 men in 1639 and 2,000 a year later to the royal army sent north to deal with the Scots. But old problems were brought to the fore — not only complaints of difficulties in finding the men and money, but also fears that undesirables would take advantage of the weakened and undefended condition of Wales. Rumours were rife of a Catholic plot, a rising to be triggered by the papist earl of Worcester of Raglan Castle, and brought to fruition by the arrival of an Irish army under the earl of Strafford.

The failure of his Scottish campaigns forced Charles to call parliament in 1640 — the first since 1629 — and to give ground when it proved overwhelmingly critical of his actions and government. At the outset, Welsh MPs joined with their English colleagues in launching widely-supported attacks upon many of Charles's political, financial and religious policies. But by 1641 divisions were beginning to open and many Welsh MPs were amongst those adopting a generally pro-royal line, arguing that, in the light of Charles's concessions, attacks upon the king had gone far enough and should end. Several even tried unsuccessfully to save the dreaded earl of Strafford from attainder and execution. In 1641 most MPs expected that the remaining differences between king and parliament would be settled peacefully. Nevertheless the growing division within the political elite, some rallying to the king, others supporting sweeping parliamentary attacks upon him, raised the distant spectre of civil war. In the light of its political, social and economic condition, and its recent history, both sides might plausibly look to Wales for support if it came to war.

On 22 August 1642, King Charles I raised his standard at Nottingham — the traditional, medieval way of calling an army together. The standard blew down the following night (By courtesy of the Ashmolean Museum, Oxford).

Chapter 2

A Nation Divides

I t is easier to explain why England and Wales drifted into civil war in the summer of 1642 than to discover why Wales aligned as it did once war began. Despite substantial concessions forced from the king by parliament in 1640-1, several key issues — the future of religion, the army and the executive — remained unresolved. A clear, if dwindling, majority in both houses of parliament wanted to push ahead with reforms in these areas, to establish a completely new church organization and to secure parliamentary control over the armed forces, senior officers of state and the executive in general. Unwilling to concede further and supported now by a substantial proportion of the political elite inside and outside parliament, Charles stood firm.

In autumn 1641 news of a rebellion by the native Irish Catholics and highly inflammatory accounts of massacres of Protestant settlers there focused attention on Charles's allegedly pro-Catholic religious policies and brought the military question to the fore. There was an urgent need to raise an army in England and Wales to crush the revolt, but many politicians, fearing that Charles might use it against his political opponents at home, questioned the crown's right of command. Charles, for his part, would not compromise the king's traditional role as sole and unfettered commander-in-chief. In January 1642 the king tried to quell opposition by entering the House of Commons at the head of a body of troops and attempting to arrest a handful of his leading critics. Forewarned, they had fled. In an atmosphere of extreme distrust and tension, Charles withdrew from London and established his court at York; many MPs and peers joined him there. York effectively became his military headquarters, for by spring 1642 both king and parliament were trying to raise armies. In April Charles was denied entry into the walled town of Hull and throughout the spring and summer there were occasional violent confrontations as recruiting parties clashed and armed groups struggled to win control of important towns. Civil war began in earnest in August 1642 when, in a suitably feudal gesture, Charles I raised his standard in Nottingham.

Welsh Reactions, 1641-42

The Welsh were both aware of, and affected by, the crises of 1641-42. The Irish rebellion triggered near panic in much of Wales, particularly south Pembrokeshire and Anglesey, the areas most vulnerable to possible Irish Catholic landings. Fear intensified when fleeing Protestant settlers began arriving in Welsh ports, telling lurid stories of Irish Catholic atrocities. Welsh MPs pressed parliament to strengthen coastal defences and, back home, the gentry set watches on the coasts, carefully searched in harbour any ships which might have come from Ireland, strengthened magazines and arrested a small number of Welsh Catholics suspected — probably without foundation — of plotting to aid their Irish co-religionists.

Although the Irish invasion did not materialize, the worsening political divisions within England produced a sense of doom and gloom in Wales. In summer 1642, one Welshman wrote mournfully, 'If there be any ill coming towards us, I fear it will not be long before we shall feel it... God be merciful to our king and to his people and make this land happy in peace if that be his blessed will... These things are signs... that the end of the world is not far off; God prepare us for it'. Another predicted that England and Wales were about to become embroiled in 'perpetual warre' and would suffer horrors like those which had recently engulfed Germany and the Low Countries. But there is little evidence of Welsh allegiance to the king's cause during the spring and early summer of 1642. References to foreboding and impending disaster in surviving correspondence were rarely linked to clear expressions of support for either king or parliament. Moreover, Wales was largely ignored in the early recruiting drives, and no Welsh towns became active royalist bases on the lines of York or, like Hull, were forced to make anti-royalist stands.

Treowen, near Wonastow in Monmouthshire, a superb early Renaissance house built in 1627 as the seat of the Jones family. Sir Philip became an active royalist during the war, sheriff of Monmouthshire in 1643, and lieutenant-colonel of the county's royalist troops (By courtesy of the National Monuments Record, Wales).

Why Did Wales Become Royalist?

In the light of this, it is not immediately clear why virtually the whole of Wales swiftly came out in support of the king once war began. During August the Welsh counties sent a string of petitions to Charles, expressing loyalty, obedience and support. Charles's attempts to raise men and money were warmly received in Wales and most Welsh counties passed into the control of pro-royalist administrators. In contrast, parliament's attempts to recruit men and to appoint its own pro-parliamentary administrators in Wales fell flat. By August, all but a handful of Welsh MPs had quit parliament, many of them returning to Wales to help organize the war effort on behalf of the king. During the late summer and autumn, men and money started flowing from Wales to the king's headquarters and several leading Welshmen were commissioned by Charles to raise regiments amongst their compatriots. Within a few weeks of the formal outbreak of war, most of Wales appeared to be firmly and actively behind the king.

Historians have put forward many different theories to explain why most of Wales and parts of England came out for the king in 1642, while other areas remained loyal to parliament. For some historians, the civil war resulted from long-term social and economic tensions, a confrontation between a rising middle class of forward-looking urban-based commercial and manufacturing groups on the one hand, and the rural elite and their tenants and retainers on the other. Religion increased the divide, the militant Protestant or 'puritan' views of the 'new men' pushing them further away from the theologically conservative or Arminian beliefs of the 'old order'. According to this interpretation, Wales came out for the king in 1642 because its naturally royalist elite quickly overwhelmed an unequal opposition. It was the weakness of the commercial and manufacturing sectors and of puritanism within Wales which ensured that the country became royalist.

The Stradling family were amongst the king's most prominent supporters in Glamorgan. At least six members fought for Charles, including Sir Edward (above), who was captured at Edgehill, exchanged for a parliamentary officer, but died at Oxford in summer 1644. His seat, St Donat's Castle (below), was originally a fourteenth-century stronghold, but was extended and remodelled in the sixteenth century (Portrait by courtesy of the Ashmolean Museum, Oxford: St Donat's by courtesy of the National Monuments Record, Wales).

Despite the widespread and almost universal support of the royalist cause in Wales, a mixture of social, economic and religious factors all played some part in determining precise allegiances. In Glamorgan, Llancaiach Fawr was the seat of the parliamentarian Prichard family. 'Colonel' Edward — as he was known — became governor of Cardiff upon its capture towards the end of 1645, and he successfully endured a brief siege by royalist rebels the following February. He also fought at the battle of St Fagan's in 1648 (By courtesy of the National Monuments Record, Wales).

Castellmarch on the Lleyn Peninsula, Caernarvonshire, built between 1625 and 1629, was the seat of the Jones family. During the civil war, Griffith Jones had been a lukewarm royalist, but by 1647 he was a parliamentary commissioner. In February 1649 a sea-borne royalist raiding party landed on the nearby coast, plundered the house and carried Griffith back with them to still-royalist Ireland. He was released unharmed several months later (By courtesy of the National Monuments Record, Wales).

Such clear-cut explanations resting upon long-term developments are now out of favour with many historians. Although all would agree that a mixture of social, economic and religious factors played some part in causing the civil war and determining allegiances, recent research suggests that the picture is very complex. Some historians now doubt whether the allegiance of a county or wider region can be explained solely or even largely by the strength of commercial or manufacturing groups within its boundaries. Similarly, research has highlighted the diversity both of religious views at this time and of the response to Charles I's religious reforms at regional, county and local levels. Again, some historians now question how far the allegiance of a region was determined by the strength or weakness of 'puritanism' within it.

Several alternative theories have been advanced for Wales's royalism at the start of the war. One school stresses the traditional loyalty of the Welsh to the Tudor dynasty — Henry VII had, after all, played up his somewhat tenuous Welsh origins — inherited undiminished by the Stuart monarchs. Other historians argue that Charles's financial policies of the 1630s won considerable support amongst the pirate-bedevilled Welsh and that this support survived the troubles of 1640-42 to re-emerge in wartime. Others contend that the Irish rebellion and Welsh fears of an Irish Catholic invasion were the crucial factors, for Wales rallied to the crown in time of crisis, while parliament's actions in questioning Charles's right to control the army and so hindering effective military action against the Irish alienated the Welsh. Some historians argue that it was the allegiance to the king of just a handful of Welsh peers and greater gentry which decided the issue, for they carried the rest of the gentry with them and the masses naturally followed suit through servility or tenurial duty.

All these theories may contain an element of truth, though none by itself is completely satisfactory. Neither traditional loyalty nor joyful support was always apparent in Welsh reactions to Charles I's policies of the pre-war years. If the response to the Irish rebellion was the telling factor, it is curious that south Pembrokeshire, one of the areas where Irish landings were most feared, was also one of very few parts of Wales to come out for parliament. It is true that many common people probably took up arms, not for religious or political ideals, but through obligation to their superiors, under some degree of duress or simply for money. The propaganda produced by both sides during 1642 was largely beyond ordinary Welshmen, for it was printed in English, a language which few could read or even understand. Welsh troops were later likened to 'moles who had no eyes' and a parliamentarian claimed that 'the common people addicted to the king's service have come out of blind Wales'.

But at a higher social level, the allegiance of the Welsh gentry was not decided by the lead of a handful of grandees. The earl of Worcester at Raglan was active for the king — as a Catholic, he naturally feared parliament — and his influence was sufficiently strong to decide the alignment of his own county of Monmouthshire and of parts of neighbouring Glamorgan. The royalism of the earl of Carbery in Carmarthenshire and of the Herberts in Montgomeryshire may have helped determine the allegiance of those counties. But in most of Wales there was no single territorial magnate or gentry grandee who completely dominated a county or wider region and who could swing a region behind the king. Instead, to explain the royalism of most of Wales we must look at the views of a much wider block of gentry and at the reasons which led most of them to decide to support the crown in 1642.

Castles at War II: Attack

Despite advances in weapons and technology, a stone castle still presented a formidable obstacle in the seventeenth century. Outright frontal assault was often impossible or would have been suicidal, though surprise attacks — usually under cover of darkness — sometimes succeeded. Thus, Powis Castle fell to parliament in a night raid in October 1644, and Picton passed to the royalists on a moonless night in May 1646. Occasionally, a castle would be swiftly surrendered in response to a threat, as at Montgomery in 1644, or in return for a bribe — £200 was the price for Chirk in 1645.

But such events were exceptional, and the attackers usually had to undertake a more complex and lengthy operation. This involved laying siege to the castle, physically surrounding it and preventing supplies from reaching the defenders. During large or protracted siege operations, the attackers would strengthen their positions and guard against counter-attack by digging their own earthworks, including long trenches snaking around the castle. They were used by the royalists at Montgomery in 1644, and by the parliamentarians at Raglan in 1646, where traces of their earthworks still survive. If the siege was effective, the hopelessness of their position, impending or actual starvation and attendant disease would eventually induce the garrison commanders to surrender. Many of the strongest Welsh fortresses, particularly the Edwardian castles of north Wales, fell to parliament in this manner in 1646-47.

Often, however, the besiegers employed more active methods to enliven and shorten the siege. Attempts were made to fire the flammable parts of the building and to ignite the defenders' ammunition store. Trenches or tunnels could be dug up to and beneath the castle walls in order to bring them down by undermining or by setting explosives. Monmouth and Ruthin were surrendered in 1645-46 as soon as the besieging forces put mines in place. If the besiegers could get close enough, a 'petard' or explosive device could be fixed direct to the gates or to a weak and vulnerable section of walling. But the commonest form of attack was an artillery bombardment.

Heavy ordnance was employed against several Welsh castles, the attackers siting their guns either at ground level, often protected by earthworks, or in an elevated position, within a church tower or on town walls. The ensuing bombardment was designed to knock out the castle's own gun emplacements and to open a hole in the defences. The attackers would concentrate on a suspected weak point, such as a long stretch of wall, a corner of the curtain, the main gates or the gatehouse. Once a breach had been made, the attacking force could storm the castle, though the defenders might well surrender at this point. Thus, Chepstow was surrendered in 1645 once the wall had been breached; in 1648 the same castle was stormed after a similar breach had been opened.

Some castles fell with surprising ease. Many Pembrokeshire strongholds, for example, changed hands several times with little or no fighting. But in most cases, the capture of a castle proved a long and arduous business. During 1646-47, many castles endured sieges of three months or more; Holt and Harlech both held out for nearer to nine months. Castles were often well supplied and could be held by a small garrison, often just a few dozen strong. Moreover, heavy ordnance was in short supply, difficult to manoeuvre and often unreliable. Even once it was in place, bombardment might knock down battlements and outward-facing windows, but by and large there appears to have been surprisingly little effect on the thick medieval walls. Even castles which endured prolonged or heavy bombardment, such as Raglan and many of the Edwardian fortresses of north Wales in 1646-47, or Pembroke in 1648, seem to have sustained comparatively little damage.

A mortar lobbed a hollow iron sphere filled with gunpowder which was ignited, ideally on impact, by a slow burning fuse. If everything worked, the effects upon castle walls could be devastating. But firing required great skill and timing, for the fuse had to be lit before the main propellant charge was ignited. If the fuse burnt too quickly, if the propellant charge did not ignite, or if the charge was too great and caused the shell to burst in the barrel, the mortar and its crew would be obliterated.

When Chepstow Castle fell to parliament in 1645 and again in 1648, the attack was launched across the open Dell on the south side of the castle. The actual breach was probably made in the lower bailey wall, at the far end of this view.

Remote and isolated on the north-west coast, the royalists in Harlech did not suffer siege until mid 1646, and were able to hold out until March 1647. A mighty late thirteenth-century fortress, Harlech was the last stronghold on mainland Britain to fall to parliament.

Castles Involved in the Civil War, 1642~48

As well as castles, a handful of greater houses, smaller forts and even one former abbey were also garrisoned at some stage of the war.

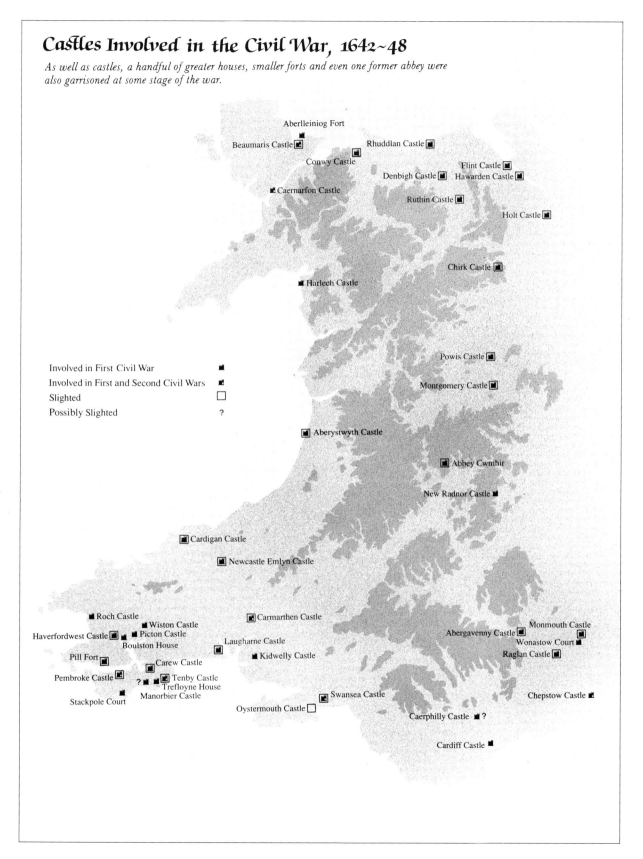

Aberlleiniog Fort

Beaumaris Castle

Rhuddlan Castle

Conwy Castle

Flint Castle

Denbigh Castle
Hawarden Castle

Caernarfon Castle

Ruthin Castle

Holt Castle

Chirk Castle

Harlech Castle

Powis Castle

Involved in First Civil War

Involved in First and Second Civil Wars

Slighted

Possibly Slighted
?

Montgomery Castle

Aberystwyth Castle

Abbey Cwmhir

New Radnor Castle

Cardigan Castle

Newcastle Emlyn Castle

Roch Castle
Wiston Castle
Carmarthen Castle
Monmouth Castle

Haverfordwest Castle
Picton Castle
Abergavenny Castle

Boulston House
Laugharne Castle
Wonastow Court

Pill Fort
Carew Castle
Kidwelly Castle
Raglan Castle

Pembroke Castle
? Tenby Castle
Trefloyne House

Manorbier Castle

Stackpole Court
Swansea Castle
Chepstow Castle

Oystermouth Castle
Caerphilly Castle ?

Cardiff Castle

Gentry Motivation

Unfortunately, we know very little about gentry motivation. Some clues might be provided by the series of petitions presented to Charles by the Welsh counties during August 1642. The petition drawn up by or in the name of 'the gentry, ministers and freeholders of the county of Flint' was typical. It praised the king for bringing 'long peace under your gracious government' and, more recently, for redressing unspecified grievances aired by parliament. It accepted and supported Charles's declared intentions of safeguarding 'the true Protestant religion in its primitive purity', the 'laws of the land in their genuine sense', the 'just' rights of parliament and 'the property and liberty of the subject.' Finally, it begged royal protection against parliament's attempts to issue orders without the crown's assent and to govern other than 'by the known and established laws of the land'. In other words, natural allegiance for the crown had been encouraged not only by Charles's soothing words, issued from York, but also by fear of disorder — social as much as political or religious — which parliamentary rule might unleash. 'Property and liberty', in that order, were the watchwords.

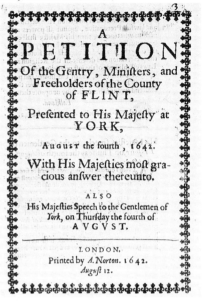

The title page of a petition drawn up in the name of the gentry, ministers and freeholders of Flintshire, one of a series of Welsh petitions addressed to the king at York during August 1642. The content of these pamphlets provides some clue as to gentry motivation in Wales (By permission of the British Library, Thomason Tract, E 111, 3).

John Speed's map of Glamorgan in the early seventeenth century. On the surface, in 1642 the county's gentry seemed solidly royalist, raising men and money for the king's army during the opening weeks of the war. But there were those who were deeply worried by the presence of the Catholic (and royalist) earl of Worcester in neighbouring Monmouthshire, and retained some affection for the Protestant (and parliamentarian) earl of Pembroke — see opposite.

Having decided to support the king, Sir Thomas Salusbury (1612-43) became one of the first commanders to raise a regiment in Wales. He saw action at Edgehill and then on the thwarted march on London in November 1642. But Salusbury's war was brief, for by the end of the year he was back in his native Lleweni, and he died there — apparently from natural causes — in summer 1643 (By courtesy of Mr Edmund Brudenell).

The two grandees of south-east Wales: Henry Somerset, earl and later marquis of Worcester (top) was a fabulously wealthy Catholic, who used his money and influence to prop up the royalist war effort in the area. Philip Herbert, earl of Pembroke (bottom), became a parliamentary governor and statesman during the civil wars. His immoral past, complete with mistresses and bastard children, was often used by royalist writers to blacken the man and his cause (Worcester photograph, Courtauld Institute of Art, by courtesy of his grace the duke of Beaufort; Herbert by courtesy of the National Portrait Gallery).

An all too rare glimpse of an individual decision is provided by a letter which a Welsh MP wrote to his sister at the end of June 1642. Sir Thomas Salusbury had decided to support the king, but only after very careful consideration, a form of mental examination resulting in something akin to a conversion experience. He had reread parts of the bible, particularly Jesus's commandment to 'give unto Caesar the things that are Caesar's and unto God those things which belong to God', and thought upon those commandments, the state of government and the church, the role of a monarchy and his own duty to his king. He had also considered the recent history of several European states and the disastrous consequences of their attempts to overthrow monarchies. As a result, he had decided for himself — 'I neither received nor sought so much encouragement from any other' — to support Charles I, feeling compelled through biblical injunction, fear of schism in church and state, loyalty to the crown, and a belief that monarchy was the best form of government, to serve his anointed king.

Doubts and Divisions

Whatever the reasons, most of Wales appeared to come out swiftly and decisively for the king during the late summer and autumn of 1642. Beneath the surface, however, the situation was both more complex and rather less comforting for Charles. Closer examination reveals that in many outwardly loyal counties, there were veiled divisions amongst the ruling gentry and a remarkable lack of enthusiasm for the royal cause. For example, from first to last Caernarvonshire appeared as solidly royalist as a county could be. But the county's war effort was undermined by a longstanding feud which had divided the gentry into rival parties, made worse by attitudes of apathy and self-interest. Although reports during August that 'the Puritans bragg of a great party' in the county and were plotting 'some designe in hand there amongst them for the Parliament' proved unfounded, Charles soon discovered the weaknesses of his own, pro-royal administrators in Caernarvonshire. By the end of October he was condemning the 'couldness or disaffection of some particular persons who prefer private ends before the publique'.

At the other end of the country, the Glamorgan gentry seemed every bit as royalist, expressing their loyalty to the king in a petition of 1 August and raising men and money for his army during the opening weeks of the war. But many Glamorgan gentry were deeply worried by the presence of the Catholic (and royalist) earl of Worcester in neighbouring Monmouthshire and retained some affection for the Protestant (and parliamentarian) earl of Pembroke, even though he had ceased to play an active role in county politics. Thus although the gentry appeared united in their support for the crown in 1642, beneath the surface there were tensions between 'ultra-royalists', many of them friends or clients of Worcester, and their more moderate colleagues, whose religious qualms and personal reservations might emerge if the going got rough. Similar divisions for the same reasons may have lurked beneath the royalist veneer in Monmouthshire. Although swift action by the earl of Worcester's son ensured that the whole county was secured for the king by the end of September, the allegiance of some of the gentry and of the southern towns of Newport and Caerleon — Pembroke territory — might waver under pressure.

The town and castle of Pembroke proved the most prominent parliamentary base in Wales — often, indeed, its only base within the Principality.

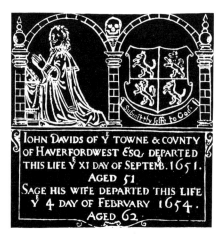

Some miles north of Pembroke, on the other side of Milford Haven, the town of Haverfordwest changed hands several times as the fortunes of the war ebbed and flowed (see p. 27). At the outbreak of the conflict, the mayor of the borough was the pro-parliamentary John David, whose brass survives in St Mary's Church. David was an associate of John Poyer, the mayor of Pembroke, who — until the rebellions of 1648 — remained loyal to parliament throughout the war (By permission of the National Museum of Wales).

Even worse for the king, in southern Pembrokeshire a group of half a dozen or so intermarried gentry families came out in support of parliament when war broke out. Based in or near the town of Pembroke — significantly, perhaps, an English-speaking area, and one with close trading links with Bristol — many of them with long pedigrees of religious or political activity and with connections to the parliamentary earl of Essex, who held land in the area, they formed an energetic and well-organized group. Royalist directives were ignored, a parliamentary administration established and steps taken to defend the area. The rest of Pembrokeshire was nominally royalist, but in the face of this determined parliamentary clique, their gentry neighbours were unwilling to take a stand, still less to intervene in the south, and were to prove remarkably pliable as war progressed.

Worse still, to the east, several Marcher counties appeared hesitant or divided in August 1642, and conspicuously failed to declare for the king upon the outbreak of war. Parliamentary hopes of securing the whole region were soon dashed by determined royalist action, but parliament did hold the southern Marches — Gloucestershire, Herefordshire and much of Worcestershire — during the opening weeks of the war and might be able to turn the neutralism and uncertainty in Cheshire and the surrounding area to its advantage. Possession of the Marches would not only disrupt royalist communications between Wales and the king's territories in England, but might also threaten the fringes of Wales itself. The eastern, lowland part of Denbighshire appeared particularly vulnerable, for the town of Wrexham contained many whose support for the crown was in doubt, and the area around Chirk was dominated by the parliamentarian Myddleton family. Despite the overwhelming, visible royalism of Wales in late summer 1642, its allegiance could never be taken for granted, and would be tested to breaking point and beyond by four years of bloody war.

A royal commission of array, issued for Merionethshire in February 1643 and appointing around fourteen commissioners. Like all such commissions, it is written in Latin on parchment and bears the Latinized signature of Charles I ('Carolus R'). The document would originally have borne the great seal, but it has since become lost. Commissioners were gentry known or thought to be sympathetic to the royalist cause, and were to encourage their county to contribute men, money and equipment to support the king's army (By courtesy of the National Library of Wales, Peniarth Deeds and Documents, Ms. 501)

Royalist ▢

Parliamentarian ▢

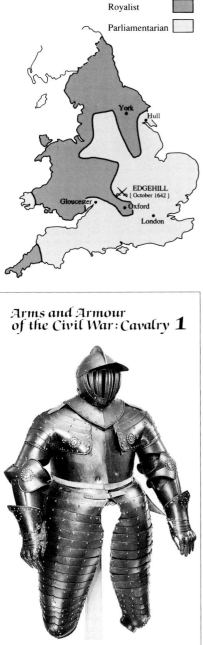

Arms and Armour of the Civil War: Cavalry 1

Royal Armouries II.198

The armour of a mounted cuirassier. By the seventeenth century the armour for the lower legs was usually discarded. Indeed, the cuirassier was going out of fashion by the time of the civil war, in part because battlefield strategy now favoured fast moving light cavalry. This trend was assisted by the cost of armour, the discomfort it caused and the fact that advances in musket design meant that even some heavier armour could be pierced by bullets (By courtesy of the Board of Trustees of the Royal Armouries).

Chapter 3

Wales goes to War

Charles I's initial objective in August 1642 was simple — to raise an army large enough swiftly to overwhelm the forces which parliament was gathering, preferably in a single, decisive battle, and so regain uncontested control over the whole of his kingdom. He hoped that loyal Welshmen would rally round the banner royal, either fighting for him or contributing the money, arms and ammunition needed to supply the army. But he also recognized that Welsh defences would need to be strengthened to guard against pro-parliamentary plots or risings. To encourage recruitment, supply and enhanced defence, Wales would have to be put on a war footing, under some form of local war-time administration.

The Commissions of Array

To this end, Charles issued a series of commissions of array, formal documents appointing and empowering a body of royalist administrators in each county. Commissions for all the Welsh counties were issued between the end of July and late August 1642 and, with the exception of that for Pembrokeshire, they appear to have been swiftly put into effect. In each county, the king initially appointed anything between a dozen and thirty commissioners of array, gentry known or thought to be sympathetic to the royalist cause. Inevitably, mistakes were made, a few commissioners proved to be parliamentarians, and many more to be inactive, apathetic, or hopelessly self-interested. In due course, the undesirables were removed and additional commissioners appointed.

The commissioners, while respecting existing judicial processes and acting within the law, were to 'secure' their county by calling out and exercising the local defence forces and by ensuring that castles, important towns, magazines and other stocks of arms and ammunition within the county were placed under royalist control. Steps were to be taken to remove from office or even imprison prominent parliamentarians, though the king urged caution here. In addition, the commissioners were to encourage their county to contribute men, money and equipment to support the royal army and to arrange for their dispatch to the king in England. These were to be voluntary contributions. Although the commissioners might whip up royalist fervour and encourage recruitment and other offerings, at this stage they were not to impress men or impose compulsory exactions.

Defence and the Militia

England and Wales had a long-established amateur defence system, the militia or trained bands. All the English and Welsh counties and some of the major towns had their own militia, each several hundred strong, mostly foot soldiers, but with small cavalry units. The officers were drawn from the gentry, while the rank and file were supposed to be volunteers from the middling levels of society — yeomen farmers,

23

urban artisans, and the like. These forces were supposed to muster and train regularly, using equipment kept stored in town and county magazines. In practice, the system often came near to collapse, equipment was outdated or inadequate, musters and training infrequent and the rank and file poor tenants bullied into serving. Although Charles I tried to improve the system during the 1630s, the results were piecemeal. Shortly before the civil war, Glamorgan proudly boasted that it had re-equipped its militia with bows and arrows, 'that most noble weapon... again come into esteem'. Bows and arrows were also cheap.

None the less, the county militia could serve as a basis for local defence, and during the opening weeks of the war the Welsh commissioners of array successfully secured them for the king, enlarged and strengthened them, and deployed them to hold and garrison strongpoints. For example, in Glamorgan, Swansea was garrisoned and a new magazine established there, Cardiff Castle, the property of the absent parliamentary earl of Pembroke, was seized and garrisoned and watches were set up along the coast.

Property of the absent parliamentary earl of Pembroke, the Norman castle at Cardiff was seized by the royalists at the start of the war and hastily repaired and garrisoned. In parliamentary hands by the end of 1645, it survived a brief siege in the following year.

Raising an Army

The commissioners of array and the local militias worked well to secure and defend Wales and to supply some men and money to the main royalist army. But their efforts were on a limited scale and rather parochial — a militia was designed to defend its home county and was very reluctant to serve further afield. In order to raise the large mobile force needed to crush the earl of Essex's growing parliamentary army, the king would need more than this. Accordingly, during the late summer and autumn he issued a string of commissions to individual royalists, peers or greater gentry, empowering each to raise a regiment of his own. Thus, Thomas Hanmer was empowered to raise a regiment of dragoons in and around his native Flintshire, while infantry regiments were to be raised by Sir Thomas Salusbury in Flintshire and Denbighshire, John Owen in the north-western counties, Richard Herbert in Montgomeryshire, Herbert Price MP in Breconshire, Sir Edward Stradling in Glamorgan and the earl of Carbery in south-west Wales.

Armed with his commission, the new commanding officer would be expected to find officers to serve him and then to oversee the recruiting of his regiment. A peer, even a second-rate one like Carbery, and a great gentry family, like the Salusburies and the Stradlings, would have a pool of tenants, servants and other dependants who could be called upon to serve. When Roger Mostyn raised a foot regiment, part of it comprised lead and coal miners from his own Flintshire estates. But a regiment numbering 1,000 or more could not be raised in this manner alone and all the Welsh commanders probably had to launch general recruiting drives, assisted by their junior officers and the local commissioners of array.

There survives a vivid account of royalist recruitment in progress at the beginning of the war in a small Shropshire village, just fifteen miles (24km) from the Welsh border. Richard Gough, a native of Myddle, recalled the day when Robert More, 'a busy person in raising forces for the king', came through. A local commissioner had commanded all men aged between sixteen and sixty to gather on the appointed day on Myddle Hill. 'I was then a youth of about eight or nine years of age, and I went to see this great show. And there I saw a multitude of men, and upon the highest bank of the hill I saw this Robert More standing,

Roger Mostyn was just nineteen when war broke out. None the less, within a few months he was commissioned a colonel in the royalist army at the head of his own regiment — part of it comprised of lead and coal miners from his own Flintshire estates. Mostyn reputedly spent £60,000 in the king's service during the war and was rewarded in 1660 with a knighthood and a baronetcy (By permission of the National Museum of Wales).

During the 1630s the king authorized Thomas Bushell to work silver mines in mid Wales and to convert that silver into coins. The mint, of which no trace remains, was established in Aberystwyth Castle (above) by January 1639. It operated for less than four years, turning out coins such as the half-crown illustrated below. The three feathers to the right of the mounted figure of Charles I, and above the cartouche of arms on the reverse, indicate that it was made from Welsh silver. The open book, just above the king's head, shows that it was minted at Aberystwyth. The Welsh mint was closed on royal orders in September 1642 and the operation transferred to Charles's temporary HQ in Shrewsbury (Coin × 1¼; by permission of the National Museum of Wales).

with a paper in his hand, and three or four soldiers' pikes, stuck upright in the ground by him; and there he made a proclamation, that if any person would serve the king, as a soldier in the wars, he should have fourteen groats a week for his pay'. From Myddle and two neighbouring villages, twenty men signed up to fight, enlisting voluntarily upon promise of good wages.

In theory, the commander was responsible for recruiting, paying, equipping and training his new regiment. Only once it joined the main royal army would the king and his high command assume these responsibilities. In practice, the commander often received financial and other assistance from the outset. In August 1642, for example, Sir Thomas Salusbury set about raising an infantry regiment of 1,200 men, divided into ten companies. Although he dipped heavily into his own pocket, he also received financial assistance from his native counties. The gentry of Flintshire and Denbighshire met at Wrexham in early August and agreed to raise £1,500. They attempted to spread the burden as widely as possible 'by persuading with the Cominalty every man in his neighbourhood to contribute'. This form of semi-voluntary public subscription did bring in substantial sums of money over the following weeks.

Meanwhile, Salusbury swiftly appointed a lieutenant-colonel and seven captains, each of whom was to raise his own company of 100 men. Salusbury himself was left to recruit just two companies — his own, numbering 200, and another for his sergeant major. After securing his servants and tenants, he found it difficult to recruit more men — his captains had already signed up most willing locals and it was also harvest time, when alternative employment was plentiful. Nothing daunted, Salusbury wrote to friends and relations in Montgomeryshire, Anglesey and elsewhere in north Wales, seeking their assistance in finding recruits. These efforts apparently bore fruit, for by October his regiment was at full strength and had marched off to join the king. It was referred to later that month as '1,200 poor Welsh vermin, the offscourings of the nation'.

Money and Equipment

Without a regular, county-based taxation, money to strengthen local defences and help raise a local regiment had to come from voluntary donations from the gentry and their lesser neighbours. In the same way, the king and the royalist high command relied upon voluntary contributions, donations of cash and plate, boosted by the occasional sale of a peerage, baronetcy, or knighthood. Charles made direct, personal appeals for money and the commissioners of array also encouraged contributions. In Monmouthshire, the enormously rich earl of Worcester had already begun sending money to the king and the pattern was probably repeated, albeit on a smaller scale, in most Welsh counties. By mid October, a royalist correspondent was praising the 'abundance of plate... [which] comes daily out of Wales and Cornwall to be coined'. Equipment was collected in a similar manner, though commissioners of array were reluctant to part with the arms and ammunition held in county magazines, for they were needed by the militia to defend those counties. For example, by the end of 1642 a long-running dispute between Caernarvonshire and Chester was well under way, the Chester commander demanding that most of the county's arms and ammunition be transferred to the city, the Caernarvonshire gentry resisting for fear of stripping their own defences too far.

Towns at War

Towns were attractive targets in the civil war. As centres of population, wealth, commerce and communication, they naturally caught the attention of commanders in search of men, money, supplies or billets. Many also contained a castle or other defendable building, capable of being garrisoned. Towns were easy prey, often defended by a simple ditch and bank, a section of which survives at Carmarthen. Even those encircled by stone walls — Chepstow, Caernarfon and Conwy, for example — could not hold out for long against a determined assault. Within Wales, only the mighty town walls of Pembroke and those adjoining the castle at Denbigh provided serious obstacles. Most towns soon proved very vulnerable.

A surviving minute-book of Ruthin gives a glimpse of how one town fared. The townspeople not only had to provide men to fight in the king's army, but were also called upon to supply victuals and billets to troops quartered in the town, plus oats and pasture for their horses. The troops were often unruly, assaulting or robbing the locals, and on at least one occasion the townspeople paid them to go away and find quarters elsewhere. When Prince Rupert and Prince Maurice visited the town they had to be received and feasted in lavish fashion, and from 1644 the town also had to support a garrison in the newly-repaired castle. Much of the town's money and produce was consumed by the royalist war effort, and the age-old thrice-yearly fairs had to be abandoned. Many of Ruthin's strongest inhabitants were conscripted, the remainder were heavily taxed and the presence of the royalist soldiers and a garrison invited attack. In autumn 1644 parliamentary troops burst into the town, wrecking the street barricades and 'turnpikes' which feebly defended it, and plundering at will for two days. Further parliamentary raids culminated in the prolonged siege and capture of the castle in 1646, though sadly the minute-book records almost nothing of that operation.

The financial consequences of an attack upon a town are revealed by claims made in 1644 by the inhabitants of Montgomery. In the wake of the campaign of September 1644 — which saw the parliamentary occupation of the town and castle and the royalist counter-attack and siege — 75 townsmen, from the bailiffs and rector down to shopkeepers and ordinary householders, claimed over £3,000 for damage to their houses and loss of cash, personal and household goods, grain and cattle. Claims ranged from £2 up to £175, and averaged just over £40 a head. Although doubtless exaggerated, these figures give an indication of the sort of damage which could be inflicted in just a few days when rival armies fought for a town.

Although Chepstow Castle was twice besieged and captured, the town escaped such widespread violence or destruction. It was a thriving trading and social centre and business seems to have continued during the 1640s, despite the war and the demands of its royalist garrison. At some stage, the royalists demolished part of the bridge over the Wye to hinder parliamentary attacks. It was standard practice to pull down a couple of arches and replace them with movable planks or a drawbridge section. The parish registers record a string of military fatalities during the 1640s, many occurring in skirmishes outside the town, though they are outnumbered by 'natural' deaths — burials of old people, drowning victims, and several who perished when a house collapsed in January 1645. The record of baptisms also shows the inevitable consequence of soldiers quartered and socializing in towns: 'Joan the daughter of a soldier his name unknown but quartered in Edward Phillip's house', 'Elizabeth daughter of a soldier his name unknown but quartered in the Court House', and so on.

Situated in the rich Vale of Clwyd, Ruthin suffered heavily during the war, both from the burden of supplying the king's troops and from attacks by parliamentarians. The town's minute book records payments for clothes, muskets, coal, candles, bread, cheese, meat and beer supplied to troops quartered or garrisoned in the town, as well as for repairs to the borough defences following the raid of October 1644. Of Ruthin's fairs, the book records laconically 'the warres & troubles forced us to forgett our selves'.

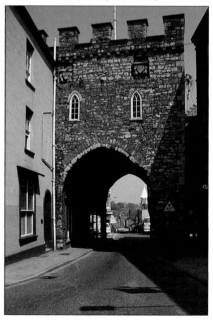

The town gate at Chepstow was the only entry into the town from the western (landward) side. The building is essentially medieval, but has been frequently altered and repaired.

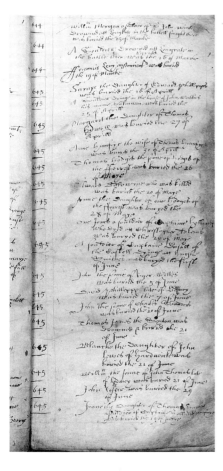

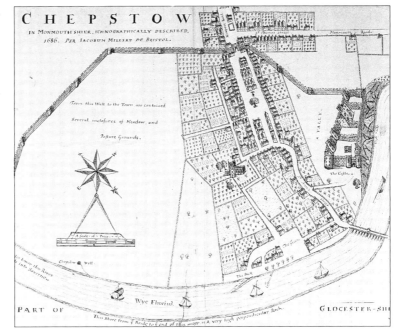

Jacob Millerd's map of Chepstow, dated 1686, shows how the town was encircled by a loop of the Wye, and — on the landward side — by a town wall. Much of the medieval stone wall, known as the Port Wall, still survives. At the time of the civil war, it enclosed not only the main street and its houses but also a large area of gardens, orchards, meadows and pasture (By courtesy of Newport Borough Libraries).

Left: The Chepstow parish register of burials confirms that, even when the war came to a close in 1645, there were surprisingly few military deaths. Of the twenty burials recorded on this page, from mid March to mid July, only two (at the top) were directly attributable to the civil war — soldiers drowned in the Wye as a result of a skirmish at Lancaut, two miles (2.9km) north of Chepstow. Two soldiers from Chepstow's royalist garrison also died at the houses in which they were billeted, but apparently from natural causes (By permission of Gwent County Record Office).

Despite its impressive castle above the Cleddau, Haverfordwest was weakly defended and frequently changed hands during the civil war. In 1648 parliament ordered that the castle should be slighted to prevent it being 'possest by the enemy to the endaungering of the peace of these parts'. The townsmen found it impossible to demolish using hand tools alone and instead asked Cromwell to spare 'a competent quantity of powder . . . for the speedy effectinge the worke'.

The large and prosperous town of Haverfordwest changed hands several times as the fortunes of the war ebbed and flowed in the south-west. The townspeople seem to have played a double game, entertaining both prominent royalists and parliamentarians during the opening months of the war. They received the rebel leaders in March 1648, holding their parliamentary prisoners in the shire hall, but then promptly declared their unswerving loyalty to parliament in May 1648 once the rebels had been crushed at St Fagan's. Perhaps because the locals were accommodating and because the town's defences were so weak that troops invariably evacuated the place on the approach of hostile forces, Haverfordwest avoided major bloodshed or physical destruction. But it did suffer financially, forced to contribute men, money and food to both sides, often enduring free quarter, and plundered by Gerard, who at one stage also ransomed some of the leading inhabitants. In summer 1648 the town provided food and drink to Cromwell's parliamentary army besieging Pembroke, and had to care for some of the sick and wounded of that campaign. The town provided 24 shrouds, at four shillings each, for parliamentary soldiers buried at Haverfordwest in summer 1648. To add insult to injury, the townspeople had to contribute over £20 to the cost of demolishing the castle at the end of the war. By then, the once prosperous town was impoverished, the consequence of military occupation, heavy exactions and disrupted trade, and the townsmen repeatedly pleaded with parliament for compensation or reduced taxes. A visitation of the plague in the 1650s added to their miseries.

Charles on the Move

In these ways, substantial quantities of men, money and equipment were raised in Wales during the opening weeks of the war. Indeed, with at least six regiments being recruited there under Welsh commanders, Wales almost took the lead in supporting the king's cause at this early stage of the war. The ambivalence of the pre-war years seemed a thing of the past. In order to rendezvous more easily with his Welsh regiments and to encourage further contributions, Charles quit Nottingham and moved to the Welsh Marches, setting up a new headquarters in Shrewsbury during September. The presence of the king and his army sealed the allegiance of Shropshire and royal visits to Chester and other Cheshire towns went some way to strengthening the very shaky loyalty of that county.

Charles also paid two brief visits to Wrexham, the largest town in north Wales. On 27 September, he addressed the Denbighshire and Flintshire gentry, gathered in the town to hear him. He praised the local people for their loyalty in recruiting troops, 'which forwardness of yours I shall always remember to your advantage', and went on to outline the wicked and unjust actions of parliament, portraying himself as a victim and refugee, a much maligned final bulwark against the tyrannies, heresies, gross injustices and unprecedented social upheaval aimed at by parliament. Charles closed by urging his audience to read and circulate his earlier declarations, copies of which he had thoughtfully brought with him. The Wrexham speech was, itself, subsequently printed.

Royalist Activity in South Wales

If the king was concentrating his efforts on north Wales and its March, the south Walians were far from ignored. Since late September the marquis of Hertford, supreme commander of all royal forces in southern England and south Wales, had been based in Cardiff. He quickly set about raising men throughout south Wales, intending to employ his army in retaking the southern Marches — Gloucestershire, Herefordshire and Worcestershire — which had been secured by parliament. During October and November he held a series of musters and recruiting drives, apparently with considerable success, for by the end of the year his army (including troops who had arrived with him from England) was estimated at anything between 7,000 and 12,000 strong.

Inevitably, the arrival of Hertford as supreme commander created tensions between him and the other commanding officers in south Wales. He certainly clashed with Lord Herbert, son of the earl of Worcester. Herbert held no formal commission but, backed by his father's power and money, he had acted vigorously during September, securing Monmouthshire for the king and raising troops. A peace-maker sent by the king reported optimistically that 'upon a small piece of surgery... do now hope I have taken away the bone that was between' Herbert and Hertford.

In order to encourage the flow of men and money from south Wales, Charles dispatched his young son, Charles, prince of Wales, to Raglan Castle to meet the local gentry. The prince was received with great pomp, fulsome speeches and costly gifts, donations and promises. On his return journey through Radnorshire, he was loaded with more 'presents', plate from the rich, 'young kids, sheep, calves,

Charles, prince of Wales (the future King Charles II, 1660-85), painted by William Dobson. The painting may commemorate the twelve year old prince's minor participation in the battle of Edgehill. If so, it dates from very soon after his visit to Raglan and other parts of south Wales. He was sent to the area by his father to meet the local gentry and to encourage the flow of men and money for the royal army (By courtesy of the Scottish National Portrait Gallery).

fish and fowl of all sorts' from 'the common people'. Everywhere he responded briefly but effectively, praising the 'great minds, the true affections and meanings of the ancient Britaines', thanking them for their 'love... bounty, and liberal entertainment' and promising unfailing favour.

Welshmen go into Battle

The troops raised in Wales during 1642 were intended for action in England. Several Welsh regiments and their commanders had already joined the main royal army when it clashed with the earl of Essex's parliamentary forces on 23 October on an open plain below Edgehill, Warwickshire. The Welsh troops did not perform conspicuously well, allegedly breaking quickly under attack and turning tail, though parliamentary prejudice may lie behind many of the subsequent comments, including a scurrilous ditty on the woeful performance of 'poor Taffy'. William Herbert, the royalist MP for Cardiff, perished at Edgehill, and Sir Edward Stradling was amongst the captured.

The marquis of Hertford's south Wales army, like several other Welsh regiments, was still being raised in October and took no part at Edgehill. It did, however, engage during November in a series of raids and counter-raids against parliamentary troops based in the southern Marches, particularly those of the earl of Stamford. Contemporary pamphlets, published in London, describe two great victories in pitched battles which Stamford scored over Hertford at this time. There is, for example, a detailed account of a battle fought near Tewkesbury in mid November, at which Hertford's 'wild Welshmen', 'poor misled creatures... as so many asses to the slaughter', were crushed by Stamford. A total of 2,500 Welshmen were slain, 1,200 more captured and the rest put 'to shameful flight'. But the two accounts are not confirmed by any surviving local documentation, including Stamford's own military dispatches, and were probably complete inventions or wildly inflated descriptions of unsuccessful raids, published in London for propaganda purposes.

Cogan Pill, Glamorgan, the sixteenth-century hall-house of the Herbert Family. Following the death of William Herbert, the royalist MP for Cardiff, at the battle of Edgehill, the family moved to Cardiff. Cogan Pill became a farmhouse until it was restored by Lord Bute about 1850 (By courtesy of the National Monuments Record, Wales).

The title page of a London-printed pamphlet, produced during the winter of 1642-43 and intended to poke fun at the king's Welsh troops. The four soldiers — Up Morgan, Up Shinkin, Maurice and Taffie — are shown in comic, antiquated dress. The accompanying text not only mocks the Welsh as stupid and cowardly, but also satirizes standard military drills in a pornographic manner (By permission of the British Library, Thomason Tract, E 89. 3).

A contemporary print of the battle of Edgehill (23 October 1643), showing several blocks of pikemen. In the foreground, two stands of pikemen are engaging. In the background, two cavalry units are charging each other (By courtesy of the Ashmolean Museum, Oxford).

The Welch-Mans
COMPLEMENTS:
OR,
The true manner how *Shinkin* woed his Sweet-heart *Maudlin* after his return from K E N T O N Battaile.

'Also fair *Maudlins* Reply and anfwer to all *Shinkins* Welch Complements, full of merry wit and pleafant mirth.

1642 · Printed at London, 1643 March 4

London-based pamphleteers enjoyed mocking Wales and the Welsh during the 1640s. Wales was a land full of sheep, leeks and toasted cheese, inhabited by comic figures with funny names, such as Thomas ap Shinkin and Shon ap Shones, and who spoke with a humorous accent. The men were usually referred to in the female form — 'she' and 'her'. They were utter cowards, terrified by battle and often running away. The Welch-Mans Complements (above) of 1643 recounts how one Welsh soldier, newly-returned from Edgehill, unsuccessfully wooed his sweetheart, offering her Welsh wine and ale and 'mountains' of toasted cheese. She dismisses him as a 'Welsh goat' and even refuses a final kiss because 'your breath smells of toasted cheese'. The Welsh-Mans Publique and Hearty Sorrow and Recantation (below) of 1647 is a mock apology by the Welsh, explaining how they had been misled by the king. The title page satirizes their strange appearance and clothes (By permission of the British Library, Thomason Tract, E 91, 30; E 378, 6).

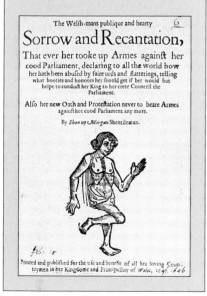

The Welfh-mans publique and hearty
Sorrow and Recantation,
That ever her tooke up Armes againft her cood Parliament, declaring to all the world how her hath been abufed by faire urds and flatterings, telling what booties and honours her fhould get if her would but helpe to conduct her King to her crete Councell the Parliament.

Alfo her new Oath and Proteftation never to beare Armes againfthee cood Parliament any more.

By Shon ap Morgan Shentileman.

Printed and publifhed for the ufe and benefit of all her loving Countrymen in her Kingdome and Principallity of *Wales,* 1645, 1646

Good News and Bad

At the end of 1642, Charles could feel satisfied with developments in Wales. Pro-royalist administrations were in place almost everywhere. In every county bar one the local militia and all strongpoints had been secured for the crown, and the Welsh people had responded enthusiastically to requests for men, money and equipment. At least six complete regiments had been raised in Wales and had joined the main royalist army in England, and during the first week of 1643 the marquis of Hertford led his army out of south Wales to join the king at Oxford. More than 10,000 Welshmen had taken up arms for the king and marched off to fight for him. Shropshire and Chester seemed to have been secured for the crown and, on Charles's orders, Chirk Castle, home of the absent parliamentarian, Sir Thomas Myddleton, was seized without serious resistance in January 1643, so securing the eastern fringes of Denbighshire. With royalist forces to his east, north and west, the earl of Stamford evacuated Hereford and Worcester during the closing weeks of 1642 and withdrew to Gloucester. Royalists promptly moved in and secured most of the southern Marches unopposed.

There were, however, a few clouds on the horizon. There had been squabbles between commanding officers and tension between the local interests of the county-based administrators and the wider demands of regional commanders. Many commissioners of array had proved themselves to be inefficient or worse, and the rather clumsy system of relying upon voluntary contributions could not sustain a prolonged war effort. If the southern Marches — Gloucestershire excepted — had fallen to the king towards the end of the year, the reverse had happened in the north. With the departure of Charles and the main royal army, the old neutralist or pro-parliamentary feelings bubbled up again in much of Cheshire, and the king's men soon found that they effectively controlled only Chester and the western parts of the county.

In only one area, however, had there been a major royalist failure — Pembrokeshire. Here, many gentry responded, not to the king's commission of array, but to a parliamentary order of mid August appointing sixteen local baronets and esquires as commissioners for the county. They were empowered to muster and exercise the militia, secure arms, magazines and all strongpoints, liaise with JPs in the prosecution of likely opponents and troublemakers and generally ensure that the county remained loyal to parliament. The towns and castles of Pembroke, Tenby and Haverfordwest seemed to be under parliamentary control. But their loyalty was not tested during 1642, for neither the marquis of Hertford nor the local royalist commander, the earl of Carbery, intervened. The over-riding aim at this stage was to raise troops and send them into England to help Charles retake his kingdom. South Pembrokeshire was an unwelcome distraction and, for the moment, the isolated pocket of parliamentary poison was left to fester.

England and Wales: Autumn 1643

Royalist ▮·

Parliamentarian ▯◂

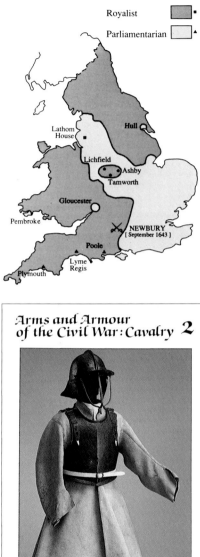

Lathom House

Hull

Lichfield

Ashby

Tamworth

Gloucester

Pembroke

NEWBURY
[September 1643]

Poole

Lyme Regis

Plymouth

Arms and Armour of the Civil War: Cavalry 2

Royal Armouries III.1942, 1976, 2021, IV.887

The light armour of a mounted harquebusier. Harquebusiers usually wore back and breast plates, and sometimes in addition a metal elbow gauntlet for the left forearm and hand. A variety of clothes were worn beneath this armour, and by no means all harquebusiers donned the traditional long leather buff coat of the type shown here. Occasionally, a trooper might dispense with body armour altogether and rely upon a buff coat alone. They also wore open style helmets, with one or more bars protecting the face. Almost all the cavalry units raised during the 1640s were of harquebusier type. They were the standard cavalrymen of the civil war — well-armed, mobile troops who could attack at speed and break their opponent's cavalry, or tear into the enemy infantry (By courtesy of the Board of Trustees of the Royal Armouries).

Chapter 4

Royalist Consolidation 1643

To the surprise of many, the civil war was not settled within weeks and both sides began 'digging in'. King and parliament spent 1643 raising troops, strengthening their hold on parts of the country, attempting to take more territory, and improving their local, county-based administrations. In the Welsh context, the royalists would seek to consolidate their existing hold over most of the country and perhaps strike at their enemies in Pembrokeshire, Gloucestershire and Cheshire. The parliamentarians, largely on the defensive during 1643, might try to take the initiative by reinforcing Pembrokeshire by sea or by launching land-based attacks into Wales.

The Royalist Administration

An increasing burden fell upon the commissioners of array, or commissioners 'for the guarding [of] the county', as they were renamed in some counties. Their main role was financial, not only encouraging the voluntary loans and donations upon which Charles continued to rely, but also overseeing new, regular, monthly levies which the king urged his supporters in each county to impose upon themselves to pay for their own defence — to support the local militia and garrisons and also any regiments of the field army stationed in the area. A meeting of the commissioners and other gentry would agree to levy a county tax and set the rate. JPs and constables would then decide individual assessments and collect the money. But the onerous tasks of overseeing the system, hearing complaints and appeals, and keeping or auditing the accounts fell to the commissioners. They also took the blame when receipts fell short. With varying degrees of enthusiasm and success, most Welsh counties imposed a local tax during 1643. Further money could be raised from the estates of known 'delinquents', that is parliamentarians in arms against the king. Their lands and buildings were seized and administered by the commissioners or their appointees, and the returns from the rents, leases and all other incomes were used to help finance the war. Numerous Welsh estates suffered in this way during the war, the most notable, perhaps, being those of the earl of Pembroke in Glamorgan and Monmouthshire.

The commissioners also exercised increasing military duties. During 1643 more Welsh towns and castles were garrisoned, more watches were set up over coasts and creeks, more men were called upon to defend Chester and the eastern borders of Denbighshire and Flintshire and to besiege Gloucester, and more infantry regiments were raised in Wales. Whether the additional troops were to belong to the county militia or to the regular field armies, the county commissioners were expected to assist in recruiting, equipping, feeding and paying them. As the flow of volunteers became ever slower, the element of duress increased and by the end of the year royalist commissioners in many English and Welsh counties were resorting to impressment.

31

Aristocrats in Command

The king also needed a more rational military command structure in Wales and its Marches. He appointed three senior officers for Wales during the opening weeks of 1643, commissioned as lieutenant-generals in April. Edward Somerset, Lord Herbert, son of the earl of Worcester of Raglan Castle, was given command over Breconshire, Glamorgan, Radnorshire, Monmouthshire and Herefordshire. Herbert nominally retained this commission until March or April 1644, though in practice from mid June 1643 command passed to his colonel-general, Sir William Vavasour, an experienced English officer. Richard Vaughan, earl of Carbery, of Golden Grove in Carmarthenshire, was given command of Carmarthenshire, Cardiganshire and Pembrokeshire. He, too, served until April 1644. Herbert and Carbery were natives of the region they commanded. As there were no north Walian peers of sufficient standing, the six counties of north Wales, plus Cheshire, Shropshire and Worcestershire, were put in the hands of Arthur, Lord Capel, a Hertfordshire peer. He was replaced just before Christmas 1643.

The three new commanders of 1643 (and, by delegation, Vavasour) were empowered to run their regions, raise new regiments and remove remaining parliamentarians. In practice, they all actively engaged their enemies during 1643, each focusing on a town or city. Carbery's main goal was Pembroke, the only secure, parliamentary stronghold in Wales, Herbert's and Vavasour's Gloucester, a parliamentary outpost which threatened communications between south Wales and the royalist headquarters in Oxford. In contrast, Capel's main task was defensive, to hold the increasingly beleaguered royalist city of Chester. Men, money and supplies from most of north Wales were channelled into Chester, for the city was seen as a vital bulwark against parliamentary invasion of Wales. In autumn 1642, one of the Caernarvonshire commissioners had urged his colleagues to support Chester, for 'if this town be lost, all Wales will be noe better than lost'. Capel repeated this theme many times during 1643, urging north Walian commissioners to support the city in their own interests and becoming increasingly exasperated at their failure to supply the promised troops and money.

The Irish Sea and Irish Troops

Besides its value in the land war, Chester was also important as a naval base. Although the parliamentarians generally had naval superiority in the civil war, at this stage royalist vessels controlled the north and west coasts of Wales and the Irish sea. Throughout 1643-44 royal ships plied these waters, using Chester and Beaumaris as their principal harbours. Prominent were Captain Thomas Bartlett of the 100 ton *Confidence* and Captain John Bartlett of the *Swan*, a formidable, newly built warship of 200 tons. Supported by armed merchant ships and smaller vessels under Captain Baldwin Wake, the Barletts dominated the area. Captain Danske's parliamentary squadron in Liverpool was no match for these ships, and although their occasional appearance off Anglesey or the north Wales coast alarmed the locals, royalist control was complete.

Naval dominance was vital to the royalists. It meant that they could move supplies quickly and easily around the coast, particularly in and out of Chester. But far more important, it might enable the king to bring in reinforcements from overseas. During 1643 Charles made a

Edward Somerset (1601-67), styled Lord Herbert at the time of the civil war. He succeeded his father in 1646 to become second marquis of Worcester (Photograph, Courtauld Institute of Art, by courtesy of his grace the duke of Beaufort).

Richard Vaughan (c.1600-86), second earl of Carbery. He was created Knight of the Bath in 1625, and served as Lord President of the Marches 1660-72 and as a Privy Councillor 1661-79 (By courtesy of Carmarthen Museum).

Arthur Capel (1604-49), created Baron Capel of Hadham by Charles I in August 1641. A detail from a family group painted by Cornelius Johnson (By courtesy of the National Portrait Gallery).

Although most of Herbert's royalists were killed or captured at Highnam in March 1643, some managed to get clear. One party fled north, along the Leadon valley, only to be caught and cut down by the parliamentarians around Barber's Bridge, near Tibberton. The buried remains of many of these troops were discovered in the nineteenth century and a monument, made in part out of stone from the old town walls of Gloucester, now marks the spot where the Welsh royalists fell.

peace treaty or truce with the Irish Catholics, so freeing the English and Welsh troops who had since 1641 been stationed in Ireland fighting the Catholic rebels. His over-riding ambition now was to ship many thousands of these seasoned troops back to the mainland, where they could fight for him against parliament. Hence control of the waters between Ireland and Wales and of suitable landing places was vital to the king's cause. As the year wore on, Charles and Capel waited expectantly, the parliamentarians fearfully, for royalist troops from Ireland to start arriving at Chester or at other points along the coast of north Wales.

'The Mushroom Army': Herbert and Vavasour in the South-East

Although Lord Herbert had been active in the king's cause since the outbreak of war, Charles had held back from granting him a commission or other command on religious grounds, for Herbert was a Catholic. The king feared that if he favoured papists, he would alienate his supporters and comfort his enemies. None the less, by 1643 Charles judged these dangers outweighed by the advantages of giving command to a proven and powerful local peer. Herbert's aged father, the fabulously wealthy Henry Somerset, earl of Worcester, had already spent prodigiously in the king's cause. The appointment of his son as a regional commander would ensure that the purse stayed open. To make doubly sure, Charles created Worcester a marquis at the same time. In terms of financial benefit, Herbert's appointment lived up to expectations and most of the campaigns in his region during 1643 seem to have been financed in part or in whole by his father. In military terms, Herbert proved a disappointment.

Lord Herbert already had a large 'private' army of his own, but, armed with the king's commission and his father's money, he set about recruiting more men. His region was well blessed with timber, coal and metals, ironworks and gunpowder factories. In Welsh terms, it was quite prosperous and the Glamorgan commissioners had been able to build up large stores of ammunition and food during the winter, upon which Herbert might draw. But this is where his problems started. In addition to the usual internal disputes amongst commissioners, Herbert found himself strongly opposed on personal and religious grounds by parties within the Glamorgan and Monmouthshire commissions. Opposition may have extended wider, for in April a courtier noted 'the Welchmen (we hear) would not rise in Monmouthshire because my Lord Herbert had the command of that county, and professed that they had rather perish than be under the power of a papist'.

None the less, by February 1643 Herbert felt sufficiently strong and secure to take to the field. Leaving some forces behind to guard south Wales, he led 1,500 foot and 500 horse against the parliamentary stronghold of Gloucester. He swept through the Forest or Dean, throwing back a parliamentary unit in Coleford, but found Gloucester strongly defended and set up a temporary headquarters in Highnam, on the north bank of the Severn. A parliamentary force under Sir William Waller was ferried across the Severn downstream of Highnam on 24 March, and fell upon the royalist camp at dawn. Some of the Gloucester garrison marched out to join the attack. Surprised and short of ammunition, the Welsh forces surrendered *en masse*. It was a blow from which Herbert never really

The lower stretches of the Wye formed a very effective barrier between England and Wales. There were two bridges over the lower river in the seventeenth century, at Chepstow and Monmouth, and so these guarded the only land routes into south Wales. Both fell to Waller in April 1643, though parliamentary control was brief. Indeed, although he took Chepstow town and bridge, it is not clear whether he captured the mighty castle perched on the river cliff (above left). Monmouth stood at the confluence of two rivers and guarded two vital bridges — to the east, the Wye bridge, and to the south-west, the Monnow bridge with its late thirteenth-century gatehouse (above right).

Sir William Waller (1597-1668) was active for parliament in southern and south-west England during the early years of the war. The campaign of March-May 1643 was his only foray into Wales and the Marches. A political moderate, he fell from grace after the war and was viewed with suspicion by his more radical former colleagues. He spent several months imprisoned in Windsor Castle. This portrait is probably a slightly later copy of one painted around 1649, during his period of imprisonment (By courtesy of the National Portrait Gallery).

recovered. The royalist, Edward Hyde, earl of Clarendon, was particularly scathing, dismissing Herbert's 'mushrump [mushroom] army' as a waste of men and money.

Herbert, not present at Highnam, fled west with his father to Swansea, intending to take boat if threatened. Waller advanced into Monmouthshire in early April, taking Newnham, Ross, Usk, Monmouth and Chepstow without serious resistance. But, fearful of becoming isolated and aware that a royalist force was marching from England to intercept him, he pushed no further west. Instead, laden with captured goods, he fell back on Gloucester, clashing with some of the royalists around Little Dean. Waller mounted a couple more daring expeditions in the area, raiding Hereford on 25 April and taking a rich haul of plunder and prisoners, but failing to repeat the trick at Worcester the following month. Soon after, he left the area for good.

Although nominally still in command, Herbert was now discredited and inactive, and effective command passed to Sir William Vavasour. In August, Vavasour led the bulk of his forces, anything up to 4,000 men, to lay siege to Gloucester. His Welsh troops sealed up the western side of the city, while the king and the main royal army encircled the English side. According to a contemporary report, Charles frequently toured the besieging forces and 'did rejoyce much at the Welshmen for they did throw their caps and hallow much with joye'. But the joy soon ended, for the approach of a large parliamentary army under the earl of Essex forced the abandonment of the siege. Vavasour and his men then joined in the pursuit of Essex's army back towards London and fought in the indecisive battle of Newbury.

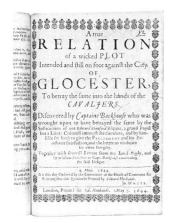

Returning to south Wales in October, Vavasour attempted a rather half-hearted blockade of Gloucester during the autumn and winter and was also strung along for weeks by a spurious 'plot' to betray the city. The tale was subsequently printed, whereupon Vavasour's stock sank still lower. At the end of the winter, Lord Herbert announced that he would stand down and make way for a new commander, but only on condition that Vavasour should also go. Personal jealousies and suspicions seem to have poisoned their relationship from the outset. Accordingly, in March or April 1644, Lord Herbert resigned and Sir William Vavasour was sacked.

From November 1643 to February 1644, one of the parliamentary officers in Gloucester — Captain Backhouse — corresponded with Vavasour, supposedly plotting to betray the city. In reality, Backhouse seems to have been playing a double game from the outset, working with the governor of Gloucester in an attempt to lure Vavasour into an ambush. This is a title page of a pamphlet produced in 1644 on the 'plot' (by permission of the British Library, Thomason Tract, E 45, 12).

A portrait of John Williams (1582-1650), archbishop of York (By courtesy of the master and fellows, St John's College Cambridge).

'An Unfortunate Commander': Capel in the North-East

Arthur, Lord Capel, commanded a region of Wales entirely free from parliamentary control. Not an acre of his Welsh counties was in parliament's hands when he took up his commission early in 1643, nor when he laid it down at the end of the year. If he occasionally clashed with the county commissioners, Capel was at least blessed with some very able administrators, men like the Bulkeleys on Anglesey, striving hard in the king's cause in order to eclipse their local rivals, and John Williams, the exiled archbishop of York, back in his native Conwy, busily refortifying that castle and several others.

The Welsh counties under Capel's command may not have been particularly prosperous, but there were coal and metal mines in Flintshire, plus the ironworks of Shropshire. At first, gunpowder was a problem, but by the summer Capel had engaged one Robert Dolben to manufacture powder according to the best available recipes.

Archbishop Williams was a rather prickly character who was often in dispute with fellow royalists in north Wales. None the less, in 1642 he devoted a great deal of time and money to strengthening north Walian castles and to bolstering support for the king in the region. He was a native of Conwy, and lavished funds upon the repair and refortification of Edward I's great stronghold, seen here from across the river. In 1645 he wrote, 'from the bare walls, I have repaired, victualed and supplied it with ammunition at mine own charge'.

The Eagle Tower of Caernarfon Castle, one of the string of coastal castles garrisoned by Lord Capel. Although parliament considered slighting Caernarfon in the 1650s, it seems to have escaped serious damage during the civil war and interregnum.

Sir William Brereton (1604-61) was a very active parliamentary commander during the war, leading campaigns in the west midlands, the northern Marches and the north-west. His major goal became the city of Chester, and he showed little interest in the reconquest of Wales. The invasion of November 1643 was his sole Welsh campaign, and much of that was apparently focused on cutting lines of communication with Chester (By permission of the British Library).

Moreover, the coasts and borders of his territory were defended by a string of mighty medieval castles, past their prime, but still serviceable.

Capel's real problems occurred not in Wales but in the northern Marches. When he arrived, the parliamentarians already held much of Cheshire, were beginning to threaten Chester, and were seeking to expand into Shropshire. Much of Capel's command was taken up with raiding and counter-raiding in the northern Marches, in the course of which he generally lost men, ground and face to the able parliamentary leader, Sir William Brereton. Brereton gained a toe-hold in Shropshire and established several garrisons close to the Welsh border. But until late in the year, the parliamentarians made no serious attempt to cross the heavily defended line of the Dee and carry the fight into Wales. On 20 June, a rare parliamentary attack on a Welsh town, albeit one in the detached part of Flintshire on the English side of the Dee, resulted in an equally rare defeat for Brereton, for his men fell into a royalist ambush. But until November, north Wales was left undisturbed.

In June, parliament appointed Sir Thomas Myddleton, MP for Denbighshire, as its major-general for the six counties of north Wales. The Myddletons were a wealthy family of Welsh descent, who held Chirk Castle and other estates in Denbighshire and Montgomery-shire, all then in royalist hands. The appointment was, at first, nothing more than a paper command, for although Myddleton arrived in the area with money and supplies, he had very few troops and no entry into the solid royalist counties of north Wales. He sought the aid of Brereton, who was based in Nantwich, and of his brother-in-law, Thomas Mytton, commanding the newly-established garrison in Wem. But not until November, following two particularly heavy defeats inflicted upon Capel before Nantwich and Wem —

The women of Wem and a few musketeers
Beat Lord Capel and all his cavaliers.

— did Brereton feel able to make a serious attempt upon Wales.

On 9 November the parliamentarians crossed the heavily defended Dee at Holt, rushing the bridge, scaling the gatehouse and bringing down the drawbridge section. When put to the test, the defenders proved rather faint-hearted and many were soon in full flight rather than face the parliamentary troops and their dreaded hand grenades. A royalist garrison remained in Holt Castle, besieged by a parliamentary detachment. But most of the invasion force swept on into Wales, entering Wrexham unopposed that night.

Some troops remained in and around Wrexham, attempting to consolidate their hold on the area. The soldiers dismantled the organ in Wrexham church, taking the lead pipes to make bullets. Myddleton conducted an extremely polite correspondence with William Salesbury, governor of Denbigh Castle, reminding Salesbury of their 'former friendship and familiarity' and inviting him, as his 'ould true friend and kinsman', to 'deliver up that castle to mee'. Salesbury declined in equally polite but firm terms: 'to betray soe great a trust as the keeping of Denbigh Castle, tho' upon ever soe fayre pretences, may be acceptable to them that desire it, but in my opinion, in itself is abominable'. There the matter rested and no serious attempt was made to take the castle by siege or storm.

Most of the invasion force marched north out of Wrexham and saw action along the north-eastern border of Wales. Hawarden Castle was

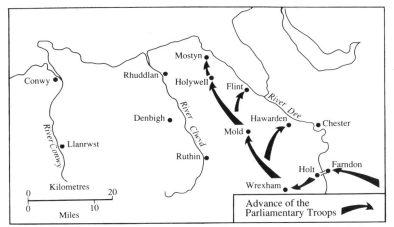

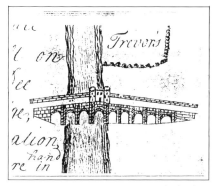

A detail from an eighteenth-century estate map, showing the early Tudor bridge over the Dee at Holt. It was defended by an imposing gatehouse, which also served to raise and lower a drawbridge section. When they attacked on 9 November 1643, most of the parliamentary army began marching downstream, suggesting that they would attempt to ford the river to the north of Holt. With the royalists distracted, a small parliamentary party rushed the bridge, put ladders against the gatehouse and cut the ropes, so bringing the drawbridge crashing down. Drawbridge and gatehouse have long since been removed, though their position remains clear in the bridge today.

The Parliamentary Invasion of North-East Wales, November 1643

promptly betrayed to parliament, and the towns or castles of Flint, Mostyn, Mold and Holywell all fell soon after with little or no resistance. By mid November Brereton controlled the western side of the Dee estuary, inducing panic amongst the local royalists. It was doubted whether the line of the Clwyd, defended by Rhuddlan and Denbigh, would hold, and it was feared that Brereton would soon strike west to the Conwy or beyond.

In reality, the parliamentarians went no further and were themselves soon in full flight. On 18 November, the long-awaited reinforcements from Ireland at last began arriving, over 2,000 of them putting ashore near Mostyn. Fearful of clashing with these experienced troops and believing that many more were about to land, Brereton and Myddleton turned tail and drew back into Cheshire via Holt bridge. Rather curiously, they left a 120-man garrison in Hawarden Castle. By 22 November, the castle was besieged by the newly-landed troops, and by further units out of Chester, and in early December the garrison surrendered. Many were taken to Wrexham, where they were allegedly 'crewelly used by some Welshmen, who did beat and wound some of them, slew other some and tooke the... clothes from other some'.

By mid December the whole of north Wales was safely back under royalist control. If the situation in the northern Marches was still uneasy, the arrival of some royalist reinforcements from Ireland and the prospect of many more coming over might remedy the situation. But Capel had proved himself a poor leader. At the height of the parliamentary invasion, Archbishop Williams noted that Denbighshire and Flintshire were 'ill united under an unfortunate commander, who never led them on to any actions, but when they were entered upon the same, he retired, and commanded them back again... and nowe that the enemy is entered these parts, dare not shew his head'. As a contemporary refrain put it, in reference to an earlier failure:

> The Lord Capel, with a thousand and a half,
> Came to Barton Cross, and there they killed a calf;
> And staying there until the break of day,
> They took to their heels and fast they ran away.

In the light of his poor record, on 19 December Capel was dismissed from his command of north Wales and the northern Marches.

Hawarden Castle changed hands twice in late 1643, as it was first betrayed to parliament and then recaptured by royalists after a brief siege. In the course of this, the royalist commander threatened the garrison that 'if you put me to the least trouble or loss of blood to force you, expect no quarter for man, woman or child'. The ruined circular keep dates from about 1280.

Churches at War

Throughout both England and Wales churches were occasionally caught up in the fighting. Large, stone structures, perhaps the only building in a small town or village capable of being defended, they might be used as a temporary refuge or as a first foothold in hostile territory. A church was also one of the few buildings large enough to quarter troops together, to hold newly captured prisoners, or even to stable horses in bad weather. Furthermore, a town or castle garrison would often place a few troops in an adjoining church, not only because its tower provided an excellent vantage point from which to spot and fire down upon any attackers, but also to deny its use to an enemy. A church was valuable in an attack, for ordnance could be mounted in the tower and directed against a wall, gate or castle. Both sides, royalists and parliamentarians alike, garrisoned or attacked churches from time to time, not through disrespect or profanity, but through sheer military necessity.

Several Marcher churches saw action. At Brampton Bryan, High Ercall and Stokesay, churches served as outposts of the main garrisons in the adjoining castles and manor houses. They were badly damaged when those strongholds suffered bombardment, and were largely rebuilt after the war. St Leonard's, Bridgnorth, was destroyed when a stray spark ignited the royalists' gunpowder store there, and at Barthomley, parliamentarians seeking refuge from a royalist attack in the steeple of St Bertoline's church were smoked out and slaughtered. St Oswald's church, Oswestry, was

In February 1644 Colonel Rowland Laugharne posted troops in Steynton to guard against any attempt by the Haverfordwest royalists to come to the aid of their beleaguered colleagues in Pill fort. A watch was kept from the top of the church tower. St Cewydd's is a medieval building, but the nave and tower were drastically 'restored' in the nineteenth century.

St Marcella's at Llanfarchell or Whitchurch is the parish church of Denbigh. It has a double nave, typical of the area. The church served as a parliamentary base and look-out point during the long siege of Denbigh Castle in 1646 (see p. 63). Bored troops cut doodles and messages into the lead roof of the tower (Photograph by courtesy of Paul Meredith).

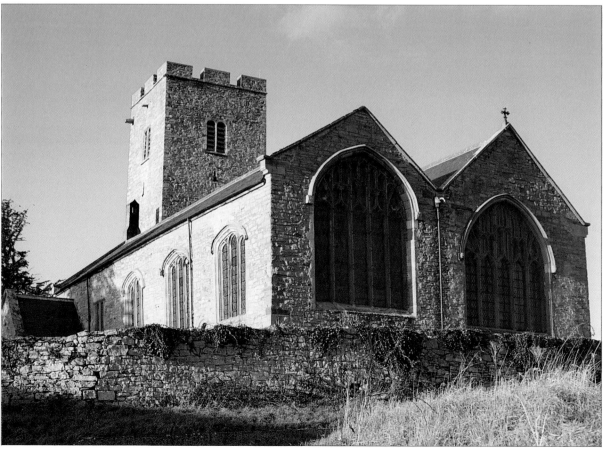

particularly vulnerable to attack, for it stood outside the town walls. The royalist garrison demolished part of the tower to deny the parliamentarians a lofty artillery point should it be captured. None the less, in 1644, a parliamentary force took the church and bombarded the town gate and castle from ordnance mounted on the remaining stub of the tower.

Within Wales, churches appear to have enjoyed a quieter war. In 1644 a parliamentary unit was stationed in St Cewydd's, Steynton, to prevent the Haverfordwest royalists coming to the aid of their colleagues in Pill fort. In 1645-46, St Silin's, Llansilian, may have served as a minor parliamentary outpost. Around the same time, St Marcella's, Whitchurch, was a parliamentary base and look-out post during the siege of Denbigh. At the end of March 1648 the Pembrokeshire rebels surprised and captured some parliamentary troops in St Mary's church, Pwllcrochan, and a month later captured more troops seeking refuge in St Teilo's, Llandeilo. But no Welsh churches endured major fighting, bloodshed or physical destruction and none seems to have undergone extensive restoration or reconstruction during the interregnum arising from civil war damage.

Some interiors were deliberately damaged by parliamentarians. Ill feeling against the master of Raglan Castle doubtless lay behind the damage to Worcester tombs in the local church, and in 1643 Brereton dismantled the organ in Wrexham church to make bullets from the lead pipes. But more common was the removal of items which the parliamentarians felt to be superstitious or idolatrous — images of the Virgin, saints or angels, wall paintings and stained glass windows, monumental effigies and brasses, ornate pulpits, fonts and font covers. To the parliamentarians, this was godly purification; to their opponents, it was wanton desecration. The historian calls it 'iconoclasm'.

It is difficult to judge the extent of Welsh iconoclasm. Although tradition ascribes all destruction to parliamentarians — often to Oliver Cromwell in person — in reality much had occurred during the phases of the sixteenth-century reformation. Certainly, Welsh churches are often plain and lack pre-civil war stained glass or brasses, though this may be the result of general social, economic and religious conditions rather than war-time destruction. But some destruction doubtless did take place during the 1640s and 1650s, and some of the finest glass surviving in Wales — the Jesse of 1533 in St Dyfnog's, Llanrhaeadr yng Nghinmeirch — reputedly does so only because it was removed and buried in a chest during the war.

A clearer view of the impact of mid seventeenth-century iconoclasm might be gained by examining the fate of funeral monuments in a single church. A series of visitors to Brecon Cathedral between the late sixteenth and the late eighteenth centuries have left accounts of what they found and they suggest that some pieces were badly damaged when Brecon fell to parliament in November 1645. A magnificent wooden monument of the mid sixteenth century, for example, featuring three members of the Games family and their wives lying on tiered double beds, was in good condition when viewed by Richard Symonds in summer 1645, but was ruined by 1684: 'there is but one large figure left thereon, the rest was sayd to be burn[ed] by the Usurper's souldiers'. The same was true of a medieval stone tomb featuring a knight in chain mail and his wife in a rich robe: by 1684 it 'hath been so battered by the late English rebells that I cannot reduce it to any figure'. But other effigies, such as those of Walter and Christina Awbrey and Sir David Williams and his wife, had survived the war unscathed. And most of the old tombstones in the floors were lifted and destroyed, not by the parliamentarians in the 1640s or 1650s, but by cathedral authorities and 'improving' architects in the eighteenth and nineteenth centuries. Despite the tradition of wholesale parliamentary destruction, the reality is more complex.

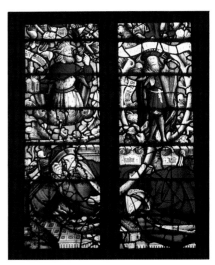

The ornate Tudor Jesse window in St Dyfnog's, Llanrhaeadr. Many parliamentarians disliked and destroyed church decorations of this kind, and this Jesse may owe its survival to removal and burial during the war years. The window shows the genealogical tree of Christ, tracing his descent from 'the root of Jesse' (By courtesy of the National Monuments Record, Wales).

The ornate wooden monument of the Games family in the former Benedictine priory church at Brecon. The monument was largely destroyed by parliamentary troops and by 1684 just one figure remained. It is still in the church, now Brecon Cathedral. The single figure which survives is one of the Games wives, and dates from the mid sixteenth century (By courtesy of the National Monuments Record, Wales).

Not all tombs and monuments were damaged by parliamentarians in the 1640s and 1650s. When Thomas Dineley visited the former priory church at Brecon in 1684, for example, he saw and sketched 'the tombstone of Walter Awbrey and his lady made with grey hard stone'. The early fourteenth-century tombstone still lies in the chancel, complete with the recumbent effigies of the couple.

'A Suspected Naturall Cowardice': Carbery in the South-West

The situation in south-west Wales during 1643 was complex and attempts to unravel it are hindered by lack of contemporary records. The new royalist commander, the earl of Carbery, seems to have had a reasonable grip upon Carmarthenshire and Cardiganshire. In Pembrokeshire, a group of pro-parliamentary gentry had assumed control of the southern part of the county. Towards the end of 1642 they reported to parliament that they held, had garrisoned and were preparing to defend the towns of Pembroke, Tenby and Haverfordwest. Yet in March 1643 Carbery was able to visit Haverfordwest, where he was welcomed by the town authorities and warmly entertained with food and drink. The reality seems to be that, although king and parliament each claimed to control parts of the south-west, such control was very hazy and, as yet, untested.

Not until August 1643 did the lacklustre Carbery attempt to test Pembrokeshire's allegiance and exert royal control. Summoned to meet him at Carmarthen, most Pembrokeshire gentry attended and meekly swore support for the crown. A show of force persuaded Haverfordwest and Tenby to submit in August and September, apparently with little or no resistance. Pembroke, however, proved to be more firmly in the grip of the parliamentarians, and its resistance was boosted by the arrival in the Haven of the parliamentary captain, William Smith. He promptly attacked and captured two royalist ships at anchor there, probably the first real fighting and fatalities of the civil war in Pembrokeshire. Soon after, Admiral Richard Swanley led a parliamentary squadron into the Haven. By the end of the summer, the position was deadlocked. Carbery controlled almost the whole county, establishing garrisons at Haverfordwest, Tenby, Carew, Manobier, Roch and a string of country houses, bottling up the parliamentarians. But he did not feel strong enough to attack Pembroke itself. For their part, the parliamentarians were isolated and, even with naval support, they were unable to break out. An attempt to recover Tenby was beaten off.

In the eighteenth century there was a strong local tradition that Oliver Cromwell in person had attempted to capture Roch Castle, but had hurriedly fled when a javelin hurled from one of the windows cut the straps of his helmet and narrowly missed killing him. In fact, Cromwell played no role at Roch, which was held by Carbery's royalists during 1643 and recaptured by Laugharne's men the following year. The castle was reconstructed and extended early this century.

Described in 1618 as 'one old ruynous castle quite decayed called Mannor Beere', Manorbier Castle was still defendable at the time of the civil war and was garrisoned for the king during 1643. The royalists not only strengthened the parapets but also constructed earthworks, parts of which remain, to defend the north-east side of the site.

Carew was typical of the castles of south-west Wales, changing hands time and again as fortunes ebbed and flowed in the area. Three times the place was garrisoned for the king, but three times Laugharne's parliamentarians were able to swarm out of Pembroke and recapture the castle. The defences were slighted by parliament after the war, though traces of civil war earthworks remain.

To break the deadlock, the royalists began constructing an artillery fort at Pill, near Milford. It was intended to command the Haven, so denying parliament a secure naval base from which to mount operations around the coasts and denying Pembroke relief by sea. Carbery was allegedly bosting that he would storm and plunder Pembroke and roll its mayor into the sea in a barrel of nails. Stirred into action, the Pembroke forces under Colonel Rowland Laugharne mounted a series of counter-attacks during the opening weeks of 1644, overwhelming minor garrisons at Stackpole and Trefloyne. The real turning point came in February, when, in a combined land and sea operation, Laugharne and Swanley took the still unfinished royalist fort at Pill. Thereafter royalist troops hastily evacuated the region and by April the parliamentarians had control of all the main strongholds, including Tenby and Haverfordwest.

One royalist officer noted bitterly around this time that the locals 'yield themselves to the first danger, or... fall in with the first protection, being very impotent for resistance in themselves'. Certainly, the royalist allegiance of the area was shown to be wafer thin and would crumble at the slightest touch. The jumpy royalist garrison in Haverfordwest fled when movement was spotted on the skyline of a nearby hill, in fact mistaking a 'herd of black bullocks' for Laugharne's parliamentarians.

Carbery was no better. In February he sallied out of Tenby to assist nearby Trefloyne, but 'wheeled about with all his forces and ran [back] into the town' when he came under fire. He soon retreated to his family estates in Carmarthenshire, and an account written around 1660 noted his conspicuous failure to crush his enemies in the early stages of the war, 'some attributing it to a suspected naturall cowardice, others to a designe to be overcome'. In April 1644 he was summoned to Oxford and relieved of his command.

The earl of Carbery (left) gained an unfortunate reputation for his inactivity and cowardice during the war. His failure to take the town of Pembroke (below) led to the loss of his Welsh command in spring 1644. He continued to give half-hearted support to the royalist cause, though he kept up a correspondence with several parliamentary peers and swiftly made his peace with parliament after the war. One acidic restoration commentator summed him up thus: 'In a word, a fitt person for the highest publick employment if integrity and courage were not suspected to be too often faeling in him'. John Speed's illustration of Pembroke shows the town in 1610 (Carbery portrait by courtesy of Carmarthen Museum; Pembroke by permission of the British Library).

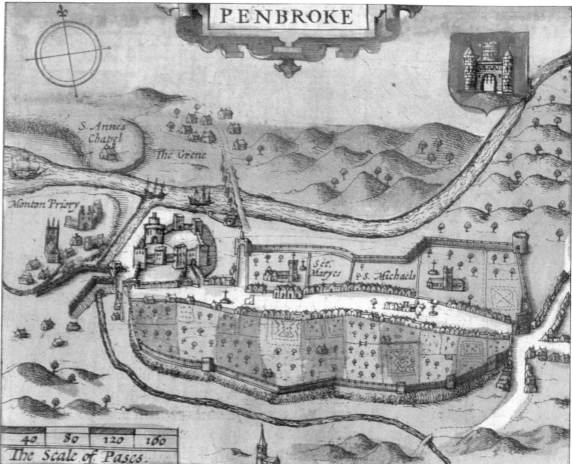

Royalist ▪

Parliamentarian ▫ ▴

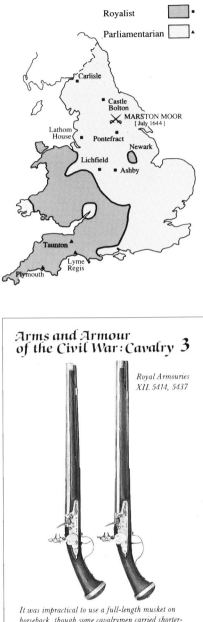

- Carlisle
- Castle Bolton
- ✕ MARSTON MOOR [July 1644]
- Lathom House
- Pontefract
- Newark
- Lichfield
- Ashby
- Taunton ▴
- Lyme Regis
- Plymouth

Arms and Armour of the Civil War: Cavalry 3

Royal Armouries XII. 5414, 5437

It was impractical to use a full-length musket on horseback, though some cavalrymen carried shorter-barrelled carbines. But the commonest form of cavalry firearm was the pistol, carried in pairs in holsters hanging by the front of the saddle. There were two main types of pistol, the difference being in the mechanism which produced the spark. In wheellocks, a spanner wound a serrated wheel back against a spring; when released, it revolved and struck a piece of pyrites held in metal jaws over the pan, producing a shower of sparks. In flintlocks (seen here), the spark was produced by a flint being brought down and striking a piece of steel. Both were inaccurate and had a very short effective range. Pistols were used in close quarter action, with the muzzle held close to or even touching the victim before firing (By courtesy of the Board of Trustees of the Royal Armouries).

Chapter 5

Royalist Reverses 1644

As 1644 opened it appeared that the royalists might carry all before them. The arrival of the first convoys of troops from Ireland and the prospect of more to follow raised hopes of a royalist triumph. Parliamentary enclaves in the northern Marches could be wiped out *en route* to victory in England; Pembrokeshire could then be picked off at will. But events turned out differently, and 1644 saw, not a final victory for the king, but a series of reversals. In England, the main defeat took place at Marston Moor in Yorkshire, where parliamentary troops destroyed a substantial royalist army and went on to secure almost the whole of northern England. In Wales, royalist forces failed to take south Pembrokeshire and suffered heavy defeats in Montgomeryshire, allowing parliamentary forces to gain control over parts of central Wales. Worse still, there were clear signs of exhaustion and mounting disaffection from the king's cause.

The Failure of the 'Irish'

In November and early December 1643 up to 3,500 English troops, formerly serving in Ireland, were landed on the shores of the Dee estuary. Brought back to fight for the king, they were promptly marched to royalist Chester to rest and re-equip. By mid December they were back in the field, the core of a 5,000-strong army which, within a few weeks and displaying a ferocity rarely seen during the early stages of the civil war, cleared parliamentary garrisons from much of Cheshire. But on 21 January 1644 the army was caught and largely destroyed outside Nantwich.

Smaller convoys from Ireland landed along the north Wales coast during the opening weeks of 1644, bringing over another 2,000 troops. But then the convoys all but halted. In part, this was due to the king's wish to retain a large royal army in Ireland. But it was also due to parliamentary propaganda and action. The men brought over were natives of England and Wales serving in Ireland, good Protestants who had been struggling to put down the Irish Catholic rebellion of 1641. Parliament, however, deliberately portrayed these troops as Irishmen, native Catholics who had slaughtered Protestants in Ireland in 1641 and who were now being brought over by Charles to do the same thing in England and Wales. The smear worked well, for many English and Welsh royalists hated and feared the new arrivals and urged the king to halt the convoys. Captain Wake, who carried many of the troops across, did nothing to ease matters by demanding huge quantities of provisions for his ships from the coastal towns of north Wales.

During 1644 parliament stepped up its naval presence off the Welsh coasts and throughout the Irish sea in order to stop the royalist convoys. Operating out of Milford Haven, Admiral Swanley led patrols strengthened by several additional ships, not least the 250 ton

Rebecca under Captain Stephen Rich. They proved very effective at intercepting royalist ships. Those on board suspected of coming from Ireland were condemned on the spot, usually unjustly, as Irish Catholic rebels. As one report of May 1644 related, Swanley had captured 'divers more Irish... whom because they were good swimmers, he caused to use their natural art, and try whether they could tread the seas as lightly as their Irish bogs and quagmires, and binding them back to back, cast them overboard to swim or drown'. This was standard practice. The king's governor of Ireland admitted that 'their inhumane throwing over board of 70 men and 2 women under the nam of Irish rebels, making the men alsoe very ferefull to venture uppon this voyage... soe that untill these seas be cleered... Anglesey can expect little (indeed noe) succor out of Ireland'.

Prince Rupert and His Deputies

As the prospect of massive royalist reinforcement faded, further provision was made for Wales to continue the long struggle. Overall military command was given to the king's nephew, Prince Rupert of the Rhine, a dashing cavalry leader and energetic administrator. In January he was appointed captain-general of Wales and the Marches, and shortly after was probably given the newly-created office of president of the same region. Rupert did much to reinvigorate the royalist war effort in Wales during the opening months of 1644, but by late spring he had departed on campaign and he rarely returned to the area.

A number of regional commanders served under Rupert. In December 1643 the newly-enobled John, Lord Byron, was appointed to command much of north Wales and the northern Marches. An experienced soldier, Byron had been active in the king's cause since the outbreak of war and was a close friend of Rupert. He was an able leader and retained his command until the end of the war. During 1644 Sir John Mennes was appointed to command the three north-western counties of Wales. A good naval officer but a poor land soldier and an incompetent administrator, Mennes set himself up in great state in Anglesey. He was soon on very bad terms with most of the local gentry, including Archbishop Williams, who alleged that Mennes and his men spent most of their time in alehouses. Mennes resigned or was dismissed in 1645. Upon the departure of Carbery, Herbert and Vavasour, the whole of south Wales and Monmouthshire was placed in the hands of Charles Gerard, another experienced soldier active in the king's cause since 1642. His lack of tact and brutality eventually led to his dismissal in 1645.

Exhaustion

The civil administration remained in the hands of the county commissioners, their tasks becoming ever more onerous and difficult. During 1644 Charles attempted to raise £100,000 to support his main army by demanding specific sums from many of his wealthier supporters. For example, Viscount Bulkeley of Anglesey received a royal demand for £120. In those areas of England under his control, Charles also imposed excise duties or sales taxes on some goods, though it is not clear whether this system extended to Wales. But

William Dobson's portrait of John Byron (1599-1652), created first baron Byron of Rochdale in October 1643. The wound on his cheek was received in a skirmish at Burford in January 1643 (By courtesy of the University of Manchester, Tabley House Collection — photograph by the Courtauld Institute of Art).

Sir John Mennes (1599-1671), from a portrait of around 1640, or just before the outbreak of the war (By courtesy of the National Portrait Gallery).

William Dobson's portrait of Charles Gerard (c. 1618-94), created first baron Gerard of Brandon in November 1645 and first earl of Macclesfield in July 1679 (By courtesy of Dunedin Public Art Gallery, New Zealand).

These three royalists ran most of Wales during 1644-45. None was a native of the area. All had military experience before the war, Byron and Gerard soldiering on the continent, Mennes as a commander in Charles I's navy. Byron proved a strong military commander and a competent administrator. Mennes, in contrast, was ill-suited to command on land and he returned to the navy in 1645. Gerard was never able to devote himself to Wales over a long period, for he was periodically recalled to fight in England. His Welsh campaigns were marked by a ruthlessness and lack of tact, counter-productive to the royalist cause.

Wales was certainly expected to provide more men for the royal army, and each county was set a quota of recruits to be met by impressment. Many of these financial and military duties fell to the commissioners.

During 1644 there were clear signs of exhaustion and resistance. The Caernarvonshire gentry petitioned the king, claiming that in the light of the heavy demands of 1642-43 and the halting of the cattle trade upon which the county relied, they were 'impov'shed... depopulated' and unable to defend themselves, let alone to supply further men and money for the royal army. In Glamorgan, the arraymen told Gerard that they could not 'apprehend any possibility how or where to find any further numbers of men as are required from hence'. A London newspaper joked that the only Welshmen not yet impressed were the arraymen, their relatives and those who could afford to bribe their way out of serving. Throughout Wales royalist commanders encountered resistance and began keeping wary eyes on the 'mutinous and disorderly' Welsh. The governor of Chepstow, for one, felt that he could no longer trust the townspeople with arms.

Prince Rupert (1619-82), count Palatine of the Rhine and duke of Bavaria — grandson of James I and a nephew of Charles I. A dashing, if somewhat reckless commander in the civil war, he was in overall charge of Wales and the Marches during 1644 and probably held the title of 'president' of Wales. In fact, after an initial burst of reform and reorganization, heavy military commitments in England prevented Rupert playing a prominent role in Welsh affairs (By courtesy of the National Portrait Gallery).

In 1644, with Prince Rupert as 'president', the land of Wales was certainly expected to provide more men for the royal army. Each county was set a quota of recruits to be met by impressment. As the months went by, there were clear signs of exhaustion and resistance.

Originally built about 1295-1310, at the outbreak of the civil war Chirk Castle was owned by the parliamentary politician and soldier Sir Thomas Myddleton (1586-1666). In the 1580s, the poet Thomas Churchyard wrote of Chirk: 'A Castle fayre appeered to sight of eye,/Whose walls were great, and towers both large and hye'. The medieval building was seized by the royalists in January 1643. It was eventually recaptured by Mytton in 1646. Repaired and renovated after the war, Chirk was also extensively modernized in the eighteenth and nineteenth centuries.

'They Begin to Warp to the Enemy': Mid and North Wales

The defeat of Byron's army outside Nantwich in January 1644 was followed by further reverses in the northern Marches. In early summer, many of his troops were called away to join the king's northern army, never to return. This depletion might enable the parliamentarians to strike into Wales once more. Sir Thomas Myddleton, on paper parliament's commander of north Wales, but in practice with no Welsh land under his control, was particularly keen for action. In late June a combined parliamentary force took Oswestry, the royalist garrison within the castle persuaded to surrender by their womenfolk. The parliamentary commanders had to call for an interpreter to translate the 'Welsh howling' of these women. Royalist attempts to regain the town were repulsed and, with Oswestry, Wem and much of north-west Shropshire now firmly in parliamentary hands, a route into Wales along the Severn valley appeared to open.

Sir Thomas Myddleton from a mid seventeenth-century portrait at Chirk Castle. Although he was in his mid fifties when civil war broke out, he was very active in the parliamentary cause both in parliament and on the battlefield. An honest and widely respected figure, Myddleton played a leading role in the conquest of mid Wales in 1644-45 (By permission of the National Trust).

Initially, the parliamentarians confined themselves to a paper war and to raiding. Myddleton issued a manifesto, promising the people of north Wales that he would deliver them from the heavy royalist burdens, restore their precious cattle trade and defend the coasts against further Irish landings. At dawn on 5 August, he and his men swooped down on Welshpool, taking a large haul of prisoners, horses and plunder. But the parliamentarians were not strong enough to attack the neighbouring castle of Powis and its royalist garrison and they soon withdrew back across the border. In similar fashion, a royalist powder convoy was attacked and captured around Newtown in early September. But it was the ensuing capture of Montgomery Castle and the decisive royalist defeat there later in September which really opened up mid Wales to parliament.

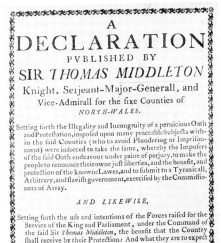

Left: Sir Thomas Myddleton's manifesto to the north Walians was clever propaganda. It suggested that most civilians were honest and peaceable people who had been compelled to support a corrupt and acquisitive royalists cause by military force. Linked with this was an offer to improve the lot of the people by removing the burdensome royalist administrations, restoring the cloth and cattle trades and preventing further Irish landings (By permission of the British Library, 100 d 81).

Below: Montgomeryshire's chief attraction during the civil war was its strategic role as a possible gateway to mid Wales. John Speed's map of the county in the early seventeenth century brings out the contrasts in the region, with many hills but also fertile valleys and large areas of wood and forest. Indeed, it was an area where timber fashioned the style of most building in this period. On 5 August 1644 Sir Thomas Myddleton's men — beginning to make inroads into the county — swooped down on Welshpool. But real advances in mid Wales had to await the capture of the key border fortress and town at Montgomery itself.

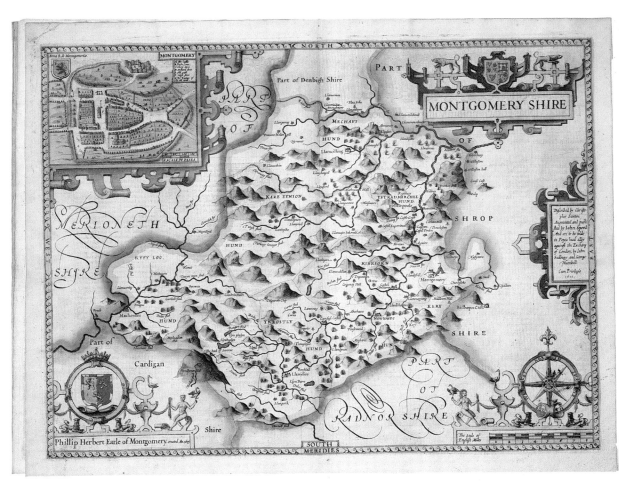

Action at Montgomery, September 1644

The town of Montgomery played a vital role during the civil war, for it was the gateway to the upper Severn Valley and to mid Wales. While the royalists needed to keep control over such a sensitive area, it was one of Myddleton's main objectives in 1644, for parliamentary control would not only give him an entry into Wales and a good base but also severely disrupt royalist supply lines. The town was small and poorly defended by ruinous medieval walls. The strongpoint was the mighty castle overlooking Montgomery from the hill-top immediately to the west. It was, wrote one parliamentary commander, 'one of the goodliest and strongest places that he ever looked upon'.

The castle was held by Lord Herbert of Chirbury (not to be confused with the Lord Herbert of Monmouthshire, son of the marquis of Worcester). Herbert was something of a renaissance man, a writer, artist and patron. He was also vain, a little eccentric and, by the 1640s, old, partially deaf and with failing eyesight. Although the medieval castle was still in good order, he lived in state in a grand mansion he had built in the middle ward. Herbert had played no active role in the civil war and, although he had attended the royal court at Oxford, he refused Rupert's requests to install a royalist garrison. In 1644 Montgomery Castle was held by Herbert and his small personal retinue, notionally for the king, but in practice almost as a neutral base.

On 3 September, laden with their newly captured powder, Myddleton and his men approached Montgomery, occupied the town and requested Herbert to surrender his castle. To ensure his co-operation, troops overwhelmed the gatehouse to the middle ward and fixed petards. Terms were agreed on 5 September. Myddleton promised that no harm would come to Herbert or his possessions, particularly his precious library, and that a guard would be provided should he wish to move them to London. In return, Herbert allowed the parliamentarians into the castle. Although Herbert remained in residence, Myddleton installed a small parliamentary garrison, the captured powder and other stores, in preparation for a possible royalist counter attack.

Sure enough, within three days Sir Michael Ernley gathered a body of troops from Shrewsbury and other garrisons and marched on Montgomery. Their approach seems to have been undetected and they fell upon the parliamentarians as they were on a foraging expedition. Surprised and outnumbered, the parliamentary foot managed to fall back into the castle, while Myddleton led his horse away to Oswestry to seek help. Roughly 500 parliamentary troops under Colonel Mytton within the castle were soon besieged, the royalists digging trenches and throwing up earthworks.

Myddleton obtained support from Brereton, Sir William Fairfax and Sir John Meldrum, and a combined force of around 3,000 men under the overall command of Meldrum approached Montgomery on 17 September. But by then the royalists, too, had been reinforced by Sir Michael Woodhouse and Lord Byron, and the parliamentarians found a force of 4,000 — 5,000 men opposing them. Leaving a guard in the trenches to watch the castle, Byron probably deployed his army on the steep-sided hill, crowned by ancient earthworks, north-west of the castle. The parliamentary army seems to have drawn up on the fairly flat ground north of the town. There was no immediate engagement and both armies remained in position overnight. On the following day, still with no sign of an engagement, a substantial part of the parliamentary horse was sent off to gather provisions for the castle. Seeing their enemies thus weakened, the royalists decided to swoop down and attack.

A bust of Edward, first baron Herbert of Chirbury (1583-1648) by Le Sueur. By the time of the civil war, he was old and in poor health, and was much more concerned with the preservation of his library and other contents of Montgomery Castle than with control of the stronghold itself.

A contemporary illustration of the fixing of a petard. A petard was an iron container filled with gunpowder, which the attacking force would attach to the weak point of the building, usually the gates. The defenders would often surrender at this stage, rather than wait for the ensuing explosion to blow the gates. At Montgomery, any desire that Herbert might have had to hold out against the parliamentarians rapidly waned once a petard had been fixed.

The ruins of Montgomery Castle. The fortress was extensively slighted after the war on parliament's orders, the reusable fittings and materials stripped out and the remaining walls brought down with explosives. Later in the century, Izaac Walton wrote of Montgomery that 'the heirs of that castle saw it level with the earth that was too good to bury those wretches that were the cause of it'.

A Possible Reconstruction of the Battle of Montgomery, September 1644

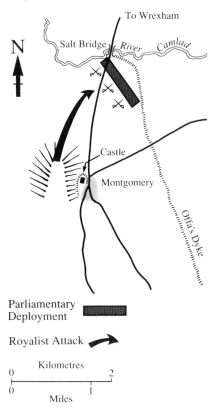

The ensuing battle is poorly documented and many aspects remain unclear. The two armies seem to have clashed on gently rolling land north-north-east of the town. The parliamentarians had the remains of Offa's Dyke and the river Camlad to protect their left wing and rear. Their right wing was more exposed and their main fear must have been that the royalists would outflank them there, and in so doing capture Salt Bridge, where the Welshpool road crossed the Camlad. Several contemporary accounts talk of determined royalist attempts to capture a vital (though unnamed) bridge. Indeed, the initial royalist attack was generally successful, Colonel Trevor's horse throwing back the outnumbered parliamentary cavalry and the royalist infantry gaining ground in a close quarter contest.

But with victory seemingly in their grasp, royalist fortunes dramatically reversed. The parliamentarians put this down to the intervention of God. Possibly the return of the parliamentary foraging party tipped the balance. Perhaps Mytton and his garrison sallied out from the castle and attacked the royalist rear, though surviving accounts suggest that they merely overwhelmed the royalist guards left in the trenches. Whatever the reason, the parliamentarians were able to regroup and counter-attack. Myddleton's horse charged and put the royalist cavalry to flight. Brereton's foot, carrying themselves 'more like lions than men', broke Byron's infantry. The conflict lasted little more than an hour and ended with the royalists defeated and in flight. One wrote that 'our men ran shamefully when they had no cause of so great fear, so that we here [Chester] are ordained to be the mocking-stock of the war'.

With anything up to 9,000 troops involved, Montgomery was the largest engagement of the civil war in Wales and one of the very few clashes within Wales which truly merits the name 'battle'. The parliamentarians had lost 40 men, including Sir William Fairfax. The royalists had 500 dead and around 1,500 captured. Several royalist regiments and garrisons had been greatly depleted. The loss of large quantities of arms, ammunition and powder further starved the garrisons at Shrewsbury, Chester and Liverpool. The defeat cost the royalists territory, men, equipment and morale. Archbishop Williams wrote that it was a bigger setback than Marston Moor, and in a Welsh context he was right. As Sir John Meldrum put it in his account of the battle, 'North Wales (which formerly hath been the nursery for the King's armies), in all likelihood will shake off that yoke of servitude which formerly did lie upon their necks, and will be reduced to the obedience of the King and Parliament by the example of Montgomery Castle'.

Powis Castle fell to parliament in a night attack in October 1644, the defenders continuing to resist even after a petard had blown in the outer gates. In the end, the fortress fell and Myddleton captured 40 horses, 200 arms and 50 prisoners, though 100 more managed to escape under cover of darkness. The medieval fortress of the princes of Powys was built of striking red sandstone and was often known as 'the red castle'.

Excavations of the ditch at Montgomery Castle have turned up a significant quantity of armour, apparently used and then discarded during or soon after the civil war. This reconstruction shows two views of a pikeman dressed in some of the armour. Much of it was old by the 1640s. The helmet, in particular, was an old fashioned design and probably dates from the mid to late sixteenth century (Illustration by Geraint Derbyshire).

Secure, now, in Montgomery, Myddleton was able to consolidate his position. During the night of 2 October he attacked Powis Castle. His men blew in the outer gate with a petard and, despite being bombarded with stones, at last took the outer ward and the inner gate. At this point the 70-strong royalist garrison surrendered. In December the small garrison in Abbey Cwmhir, Radnorshire, was taken by storm and the building wrecked. Some parliamentary troops, forced to land in Pembrokeshire, marched across Wales to join Myddleton, beating off a royalist ambush near Machynlleth and burning Mathafarn, the home of the royalist leader, Rowland Pugh. Some of the Montgomeryshire gentry also came over to parliament, the royalists noting sadly that 'the edge of the gentry is very much blunted — the country's loyalty strangely abated. They begin to warp to the enemy'. By the end of 1644 Myddleton had established a strong parliamentary enclave in mid Wales, centred on Montgomery and Powis castles, cemented by a handful of other garrisons and supported by some of the local gentry.

When he took Abbey Cwmhir at the end of 1644, Myddleton described the place as 'a very strong house, and built with stone of the greatest thickness, and the walls and outworks all very strong, the house having been in former times an Abbey of the Papists'. Following the civil war slighting and further decay, little now remains of the twelfth-century Cistercian abbey.

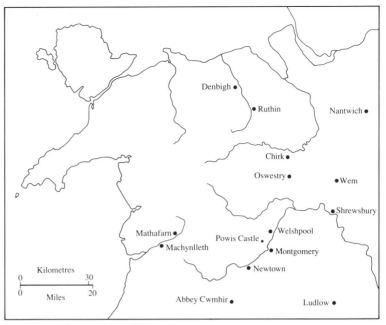

Mid and North Wales, 1644
The map shows the towns and buildings involved in the campaigns of 1644.

On the other hand, there were limits to Myddleton's success. He had few troops at his command, probably less than 400, admitting in one report, 'with what number of men I... do these things, I dare not commit to paper'. With these, he could not move far into the Welsh heartlands or take a major stronghold. Thus, although he smashed into Ruthin in late October, overwhelming the street barricades and plundering the town, he was not able to take the castle — still being repaired and fortified — and had to withdraw. Denbigh Castle was far too strong and, the bitterest blow of all, a surprise night attack and a three day siege both failed to recover his own castle at Chirk, garrisoned for the king since 1643. The royalist governor wrote that during the siege 'their engineers attempted to work into the castle with iron crows and pickers, under great planks and tables which they had erected against the castle side for shelter, but my stones beat them off'.

Requests for reinforcements fell on deaf ears, for parliament was more interested in Brereton's campaign against Chester. Parliament accorded Myddleton's mid Wales campaign a low priority and was unwilling to allocate men and money to it. Myddleton also feared that the local gentry who had come over to him were merely flowing with the tide and would happily return to the king if royalist forces attempted to retake Montgomeryshire.

'His Irish and Popish Forces': Gerard in South Wales

When Charles Gerard took command of south Wales in spring 1644, the royalists were under threat on both flanks. To the east, the Monmouthshire border was falling prey to occasional attacks from the Gloucester parliamentarians. In January, for example, they had raided Chepstow, carrying off prisoners and plunder. In September, Monmouth itself was betrayed to the parliamentarians, who established a garrison there and a minor outpost at Wonastow House, only to be expelled two months later when the royalists forced open a town gate with a crowbar and recovered Monmouth. Despite royalist fears over the loyalty of the locals and parliamentary control of western Gloucestershire, Monmouthshire remained in royalist hands in 1644 and the parliamentarians could, as yet, do little more than mount occasional raids across the Wye.

In the south-west the situation was far more serious, and it was there that Gerard focused his efforts. By spring 1644 the parliamentarians seem to have held not only Pembrokeshire but also parts of Cardiganshire and Carmarthenshire, including the two county towns. Once more, however, fortunes were dramatically reversed. Entering south Wales in May with an army of around 2,000 men, Gerard launched an energetic and brutal campaign which, in barely twelve weeks, led to the recapture of most of south-west Wales. From the outset, Gerard sought to impose his will, making heavy demands on county commissioners, dismissing the existing governors of Swansea and Cardiff and appointing Englishmen of his own choosing, and sweeping westwards to engage his enemies. Kidwelly and Carmarthen were secured, the town and castle of Cardigan were taken by force, and then in quick succession the castles of Laugharne, Newcastle Emlyn and Roch. After some resistance, Haverfordwest fell to Gerard and 'his Irish and Popish forces', as a London newspaper inaccurately but emotively called his army, leaving Laugharne's parliamentarians penned into Pembroke and Tenby.

Gerard, aware perhaps of the fickle nature of the local population, tried to cement royalist control of south-west Wales. Garrisons were planted throughout the area, many of them under English or non-local governors. He also introduced a 'scorched earth' policy, driving off cattle and burning corn, to deny supplies to foraging parties sallying out of Pembroke and Tenby. Perhaps, too, this action was intended to inspire such fear that the people would never again waver from their duty to the king. London newspapers suggested he went further, torturing and executing civilians indiscriminately.

Gerard's policies failed on all counts. They did not lead to the eradication of the parliamentarians, for when he and most of his army were called away at the end of August to serve in England, Pembroke and Tenby remained in parliamentary hands. Nor did the intense garrisoning and show of force more firmly secure the rest of the area for the king. The familiar pattern was repeated, for during the closing months of 1644 the parliamentarians swarmed forth out of Pembroke and retook the whole of Pembrokeshire with minimal resistance. Only when they tried to push further east did they lose momentum and encounter serious opposition. It required a week-long siege and bombardment, followed by the capture of its outer ward, before Laugharne Castle surrendered on 3 November. The town of Cardigan surrendered easily enough in December, but the castle there, 'a considerable place, ably manned', held out until a three-day parliamentary bombardment breached a wall. Even then, the garrison would not surrender and the castle had to be taken by storm.

But Gerard's brutal policies of summer 1644 also failed because they left an enduring legacy of bitterness and antagonism, even amongst hitherto loyal, royalist civilians. It was this growing disaffection amongst the royalist Welsh, as much as parliament's military campaigns and victories, which would spell the end of the king's cause in Wales.

Sir Peter Lely's portrait of Sir Edward Massey (c. 1618-74), a leading parliamentarian during the war, but an active royalist during the 1650s. The earl of Clarendon called him 'a wonderfully vain and weak man' (By courtesy of the National Gallery of Canada).

The south face of the twelfth-century great tower of Monmouth Castle. Part of the tower collapsed in 1647, probably the result of undermining during the civil war.

Massey became governor of Gloucester at the end of 1642 and remained in charge of operations there until summer 1645. Against all odds, he withstood the 1643 royalist siege of the city and survived repeated attacks thereafter. By 1644 Gloucester was safe, and Massey was able to mount operations further afield, including attacks upon some of the royalist bases in eastern Monmouthshire. But although the raids were often very successful, Massey lacked the manpower to establish permanent garrisons in south-east Wales and the royalists soon returned. Thus, although Massey captured the town and castle of Monmouth in September 1644, both were retaken by the king's men in November and remained in royalist hands for a further year.

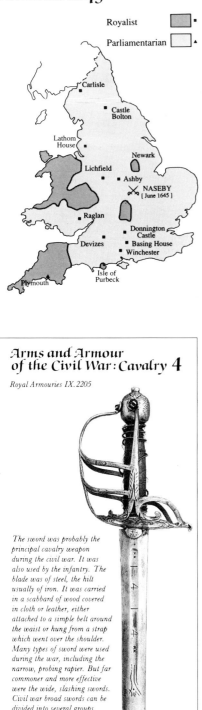

Royalist ■·

Parliamentarian □▲

Chapter 6

Royalist Collapse 1645-46

The king's cause collapsed during 1645-46. In England, he suffered a string of heavy defeats, the worst being the destruction of his main army at Naseby in June 1645. The parliamentarians slowly but steadily took control of the whole of England, overwhelming towns, castles and other strongholds. In June 1646 Charles surrendered, and, on his orders, most of the remaining bases in England also surrendered. This process was mirrored by a royalist collapse in Wales. In some areas, particularly the south-west, the parliamentary triumph was advanced by victory in battle. But in much of Wales, the key element was the desertion of the royalist cause *en masse* by the civilian population. Because of this, Wales largely avoided widespread bloodshed, and the extension of parliamentary control was achieved with little fighting. Bereft of support, a few diehard royalists retreated into castles and walled towns and tried to continue the struggle. The closing stages of the civil war in Wales were marked by a number of formal sieges.

The Irish and the Scots

The attempt to hang on to a number of towns and castles was not completely futile. To the end, some royalists cherished a hope that further reinforcements would arrive from Ireland. By this time, Charles was attempting not only to bring over more units of the English army but also to persuade the native Irish Catholics to fight for him in England and Wales. Hence the royalist attempts to retain the towns and castles along the north Wales coast for as long as possible since they might serve as potential landing places for reinforcements. In practice, only a trickle of men arrived across the Irish Sea. Moreover, the news that Charles was trying to reach agreement with Irish Catholics and to bring them to Wales provoked consternation amongst Welsh royalists. Charles attempted to shift attention to parliament's Scottish allies, who were mounting an often brutal campaign in the Marches, claiming that parliament had promised them Welsh land as a reward for their services. This parliament strenuously denied and the Scots were not, in fact, granted Welsh estates.

Welsh hatred of the Irish and a growing alienation from the royalist cause proved far stronger than any fears of the Scots. During 1645 there was a mounting tide of complaints, petitions, defections and, ultimately, open resistance. In county after county, the gentry petitioned the king and other senior royalists for redress of grievances. Most stressed that their county was exhausted and unable to raise further money and men, and went on to demand an end to free quarter, martial law and irregular taxes, the removal of English garrisons and governors, and an assurance that no more Irish would be landed. In addition, the northern counties demanded permission

Arms and Armour of the Civil War: Cavalry 4

Royal Armouries IX.2205

The sword was probably the principal cavalry weapon during the civil war. It was also used by the infantry. The blade was of steel, the hilt usually of iron. It was carried in a scabbard of wood covered in cloth or leather, either attached to a simple belt around the waist or hung from a strap which went over the shoulder. Many types of sword were used during the war, including the narrow, probing rapier. But far commoner and more effective were the wide, slashing swords. Civil war broad swords can be divided into several groups, according to the design of the hilt. The most impressive is the mortuary sword, with its large dish-shaped guard at the top of the blade, elaborate knuckle guards and generous pommel. The outer surfaces were usually decorated in a variety of patterns (By courtesy of the Board of Trustees of the Royal Armouries).

Sir Jacob Astley (1579-1652), created baron Astley during the war, became royalist commander of south Wales in summer 1645. His command was brief, for by autumn royalist control was crumbling. Astley, a tough and experienced veteran, well over sixty in 1642, played a part in many of the campaigns and battles of the civil war. His prayer at Edgehill, just before battle, has become famous: 'Oh Lord, Thou knowest how busy I must be this day, if I forget Thee, do not Thou forget me' (By permission of the British Museum).

Sir John Owen, royalist commander of north-west Wales from 1645. He was another officer who had been very active in the king's cause. According to one contemporary account, he took part in seven battles, nine sieges and 32 other actions. Owen led the royalist rebellion in north Wales in 1648, was captured and sentenced to death, but successfully pleaded his life. In July 1649, he entertained the diarist John Evelyn to dinner and to music by 'one Carew, who played incomparably on the Welsh harp' (By courtesy of the National Library of Wales).

to resume their lucrative cattle trade with England, while the southern counties often urged the dismissal of the brutal and unpopular Gerard.

By spring 1645 the local royalist commanders were becoming jumpy, all too aware of local feeling and of their own weakening grip on Wales. Rupert himself wrote 'I fear all Wales will be in rebellion', and one of his officers was even more doleful about the state of affairs in Monmouthshire. Captain Dabridgecourt found the locals untrustworthy and disobedient, contemptuous of his command and unwilling to co-operate. He snarled that 'here be two or three constables deserve hanging', though he knew he did not have the power to do this. He begged Rupert, 'if your Highness shall be pleased to command me to the Turk, or Jew, or Gentile, I will go on my bare feet to serve you; but from the Welsh, good Lord deliver me'.

New Commanders

Several royalist and parliamentary commanders were active in Wales during the closing stages of the war. The king was forced to relieve Gerard of his command during 1645 and thenceforth south Wales was in the hands of Sir Jacob Astley, a tough English veteran. In north Wales and its Marches, the continuing absence of Prince Rupert led during the winter of 1644-45 to his replacement as overall commander by his younger brother, Prince Maurice. Sir John Mennes resigned his command of the three north-western counties in summer 1645 and was replaced by a local man, Sir John Owen. Lord Byron retained command of the north-eastern counties until their fall, whereupon he held out in Caernarfon until the bitter end. On the parliamentary side, Rowland Laugharne was supreme in the south-west and the new governor of Gloucester, Thomas Morgan, began eating into Monmouthshire and south-east Wales. In the north, Sir William Brereton continued to concentrate on Cheshire rather than Wales, and Sir Thomas Myddleton was forced to resign his commission during summer 1645. Instead, the task of mopping up north Wales fell to Myddleton's brother-in-law, Thomas Mytton.

'The Gentry Declare for Parliament': The South-East

It was in south-east Wales that local disaffection first swamped the royalist cause. Ironically, it may have been Charles's own presence which triggered the reaction. After his defeat at Naseby, the king came to south-east Wales, residing at the marquis of Worcester's seat at Raglan and issuing heavy demands upon the surrounding counties for more men and money to rebuild his army. Instead, Glamorgan and Monmouthshire raised irregular armies of their own in order to win redress of grievances. The Glamorgan force, up to 5,000 men under the control of local gentry, soon adopted the title 'the Peaceable Army'. They still declared allegiance to the king's cause and even promised to raise some men and money for his army, but they insisted that a number of terms must first be met. They wanted the king to declare his support for the Protestant church; to promise to impose no additional or excessive taxes; to remove the English garrison and its governor at Cardiff, and to replace them with local men; to dismiss all papists; and to relieve the hated Gerard of his Welsh command.

With his army crushed at Naseby and the war all but lost, Charles travelled to south-east Wales. He was in the area for a month, from early July to early August 1645, and again for around a week in September. On both occasions, his principal residence was Raglan Castle, but he also dined and slept in several other buildings in the area. He was trying to rebuild his army, re-establish his authority in the area, and plan future campaigns. In reality, his position was undermined both by open hostility in south-east Wales and by news of further defeats elsewhere, especially the loss of Bridgwater and Bristol. He left the region in mid September, never to return.

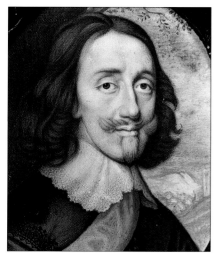

David Des Granges's miniature of the king, painted around 1645, has an unmistakable air of melancholy about it. The eyes are heavy and sorrowful, the beard and moustache flecked with grey (By courtesy of the National Portrait Gallery).

On Wednesday 16 July, the king, attended by peers, household officers and two troops of horse, left Raglan and dined at Tredegar, though they then moved on and spent the night in Cardiff. They were at Tredegar again the following day and on this occasion Charles slept there. The medieval house had been in the Morgan family for generations, and Charles's host was the aged Sir William Morgan. The medieval range, centred on the great hall, was soon to be absorbed into a much grander edifice (By courtesy of Newport Borough Council).

Raglan Castle was the king's main residence during his time in the area, for three weeks during July and for a further week in September. Formal meals and other entertainments would have taken place in the great hall, a late medieval building remodelled and modernized by the Somerset family in the mid sixteenth century.

The king stayed in Cardiff Castle from 29 July to 5 August, the week of his uncomfortable meetings with the Peaceable Army. It was from Cardiff, on 3 August, that Charles wrote a remarkable letter to Prince Rupert: 'I confess that, speaking as a mere soldier or statesman, I must say there is no probability but of my ruin; yet as a Christian, I must tell you that God will not suffer rebels and traitors to prosper nor this cause to be overthrown'. He was resolved, 'whatever personal punishment', to fight on for the good of his successors and friends. The self-created myth of the doomed martyr was already being built (By courtesy of Cardiff City Council).

According to a diarist who accompanied Charles, on Sunday 27 July 'His Majesty lay at Rupperie, a faire seat of Mr Morgan'. This was Rhiwperra, the grand house or mock castle of a cadet branch of the Tredegar Morgans. It was young Thomas Morgan who entertained the king, probably for two or three days. Rhiwperra, built less than twenty years before Charles's visit, was a grand quadrangular mansion with huge round towers at each corner. Sadly, it is now a gutted shell (By courtesy of the National Monuments Record, Wales).

Thomas Morgan (1604-79) replaced Massey as governor of Gloucester in June 1645 and thereafter was involved in operations to clear south-east Wales and the southern Marches of remaining royalist bases, including Chepstow, Monmouth, Raglan and Hereford. He supported the Stuart restoration, obtained a baronetcy in 1661 and served as governor of Jersey from 1665 until his death. Allegedly almost illiterate and barely able to sign his name, he ran military and administrative affairs with considerable skill and perception (By courtesy of the Ashmolean Museum, Oxford).

Chepstow Castle from the east. During October 1645 Morgan captured the town without serious resistance, but the castle garrison held out. Reinforcements and heavy guns were brought up from Bristol, a bombardment opened up at least one hole in the castle walls and on 10 or 11 October Colonel Fitzmorris and his men surrendered. Morgan took prisoners and horses, arms and ammunition, 400 barrels of butter, six hogshead of biscuit and 'divers hundredweight of cheese'.

Some locals were apparently vowing 'to cut him to pieces for firing the corn and plundering the county of Pembroke'.

Charles met the Peaceable Army and its leaders in Cardiff at the beginning of August. Shocked by its attitude and visibly shaken, the king had no choice but to grant their requests. He then left the area, but returned with further troops in September, determined to crush local resistance. He compelled the Peaceable Army to disband and arrested opposition ringleaders in Glamorgan and Monmouthshire. But the loss of Bristol and other setbacks paralysed the king and halted his attempts to reimpose his command in south Wales and he promptly left the area, never to return.

With the king's departure, the royalist cause quickly collapsed. The Peaceable Army and similar bodies reformed, but now they were openly anti-royalist and looked towards parliament to deliver them from papists, heavy taxes, acquisitive garrisons and other burdens. As the Peaceable Army secured control of Glamorgan, Sir Jacob Astley wrote in despair that 'the county of Glamorgan so unquiet as there is no good to be expected' and admitted that he had no power to hold the region. The London newspapers reported joyfully that 'even the county of Glamorgan, where the parliament was never wont to be named but in detestation, begins to clear up, and the greater part of the gentry declare for parliament'.

A similar process was under way in Monmouthshire. Local gentry favourable to parliament secured much of the county, though Thomas Morgan and his troops had to intervene to capture two crucial strongholds. The town of Chepstow was taken without resistance, but only when a parliamentary bombardment breached the castle wall on 11 October did the 60-man garrison within surrender. Similarly, Monmouth town quickly fell, but the castle garrison endured a three day-siege, surrendering on 24 October when mines were placed beneath the walls. By the end of October, only Raglan held out for the king. For the moment, parliament made no attempt to reduce that formidable castle.

In the autumn Astley noted with alarm that the gentry of Breconshire were 'inclined to be neutral and to join with the strongest party'. By November it was clear to everyone who that party was, and on the 23rd parliamentary forces were welcomed into Brecon. The Radnorshire gentry, too, declared for parliament. Royalist troops within those two counties had found it prudent to withdraw and there was no serious resistance to this process.

There were, however, problems in Glamorgan at the beginning of 1646. The local gentry had come out for parliament in autumn 1645, not through a love of the parliamentary cause, but because parliament's troops might deliver them from royalist oppression. Instead, they found themselves saddled with all the old burdens, now carrying parliamentary instead of royalist labels — English troops and governors, heavy taxes and religious innovation, in this case the banning of the old prayer book. Accordingly, the Peaceable Army was revived, took control of Cardiff town in mid February and besieged the parliamentary garrison in the castle. Laugharne marched to the rescue and on 18 February engaged and scattered the motley 'army' on an open heath just north of Cardiff. The events of July to November 1645 and February 1646 are best seen, not as groundswells of local support first for parliament and then for the king, but rather as consistent expressions of local independence in defence of local interests against whichever outside party was attempting to impose itself. There was a warning here for parliament.

Sir Thomas Fairfax (1612-71), later third baron Fairfax, was parliamentary commander in chief from February 1645. His supervision of the closing stages of the siege of Raglan was his only campaign in Wales. Upon arrival, he increased the pressure by deploying mortars and ordering further trenches dug closer to the enemy positions. According to one contemporary account, 'the General is every day in the trenches, and yesterday appointed a new approach, which the engineer of this army, returned from Worcester, is to carry on with all expedition (By courtesy of York City Art Gallery).

This cannon shot mould, discovered at Raglan, had presumably been used and then abandoned by the royalists in 1646. It is the bottom half of a two-part mould. The upper section would have contained the hole through which the molten iron was poured. The mould would have produced small 3 inch (7.6 cm) diameter cannon balls, suitable for the small guns which the royalists mounted in the towers of the castle.

Towards the end of the siege, the parliamentarians planted six mortars around Raglan, each capable of lobbing 12 inch (30.5 cm) 'grenade shells'. They were to induce the royalists to continue negotiations — 'in case the treaty do break off, we are ready to show by what extremity they must expect to be reduced'. 'Roaring Meg', perhaps the only civil war mortar to survive, is typical of those used at Raglan, and may well have been deployed there itself. The bed on which it rests is, however, modern.

Some of the now-decayed civil war earthworks dug by both sides around Raglan Castle are still visible. The royalists threw up banks, ditches and bastions to protect the vulnerable south-eastern approaches, along the southern side of the present car park and in the fields on either side ('A' on photograph). The parliamentarians threw up a battery on high ground north-east of the castle ('B'), a pentagonal arrangement of banks and ditches (Cambridge University Collection: copyright reserved).

None the less, after Laugharne restored order in Glamorgan, just one thorn remained to be plucked in south-east Wales — Raglan. With its strong garrison, plentiful supplies, deep moat, thick walls, and outer earthworks, Raglan Castle was a formidable obstacle. Although the parliamentarians had kept it under close watch from autumn 1645, not until summer 1646 did the formal siege begin. Laugharne and Morgan invested the castle and on 3 June they called upon the old marquis of Worcester to abandon the hopeless cause and surrender. Upon his refusal a thirteen-week siege began. Parliamentary troops, reinforced and commanded by Sir Thomas Fairfax, dug trenches around the castle, raised batteries, and bombarded the place. At length the marquis recognized the futility of further struggle, perhaps accepting the authenticity of reports that the king had commanded remaining bases to surrender, perhaps fearing the effect of the heavy mortars and 'grenade shells' which the parliamentarians were threatening to employ. After brief negotiations, Raglan was surrendered on terms on 19 August. The war in south-east Wales and Monmouthshire was over.

'Our Guns Played Hard this Day': The Siege of Laugharne Castle

Laugharne Castle stands in south-west Wales, by the estuary of the Taf. Water, mud and marsh stretch beyond its southern and eastern walls. The spot had been fortified as early as the twelfth century, and the surviving castle is essentially medieval. Laugharne was, however, extensively remodelled by Sir John Perrot in the late sixteenth century, when the inner ward was converted into a Tudor mansion and the outer ward became a garden. The castle appears to have stood empty for several decades after Perrot's death in 1592 and was doubtless rather dilapidated by the 1640s, but it possessed fully walled inner and outer wards and a strong gatehouse. As such, it was quite defensible.

Laugharne Castle played no recorded military role during the opening two years of the civil war. In summer 1644 it was secured for the king by Charles Gerard, and a 200-strong royalist garrison was installed under Lieutenant-Colonel Russell. By the autumn Gerard had left the region and Rowland Laugharne's Pembrokeshire parliamentarians felt able to move against the castle.

Parliamentary troops began gathering near the town over the weekend of 26-27 October. By Monday, 28 October Laugharne had a force of 2,000 men, mostly infantry, but including some cavalry and dragoons. He also had several pieces of ordnance, essential for an attack on a castle. The troops probably camped 'within a mile of the castle', perhaps near the main road from St Clears as it begins its gentle descent into the town (**A**).

On Tuesday morning, 29 October, Laugharne moved his men closer to the castle, probably on the hillside north-north-east of it (**B**), and he formally summoned the garrison to surrender. They refused. Laugharne may have established a battery on this hillside, perhaps making use of the prehistoric or Romano-British earthwork there, from which artillery could bombard the east and north-east walls of the castle. At the same time, 200 musketeers were dispatched to seize the town, which was probably protected by nothing more than earthen banks and ditches. By early afternoon the town was secured and Laugharne moved some of his guns nearer the castle, perhaps to the lower slopes of the hill west-north-west of the defences (**C**). However, neither of his artillery positions enabled Laugharne to fire directly at the outer gates of the castle.

On Wednesday, 30 October, a show of force frightened off two bodies of royalist cavalry seen on a nearby hill. That night, the parliamentarians

Rowland Laugharne, stout defender of Pembroke, mopped up most of the royalist bases in the region during the closing years of the war. He led the parliamentary force which besieged Laugharne Castle, 28 October to 3 November 1644. In 1648, he rebelled against parliament, was defeated and condemned to death, but reprieved. He spent his last 25 years in poverty and debt, despite royal promises of aid and from 1661 a seat in parliament. In 1670 he reportedly had 'to pawn his cloak and sword, and has only 3 shillings in the world' (By permission of the British Library).

A back plate, probably from a pikeman's armour, as found during excavations in the post civil war demolition deposits at Laugharne Castle (By courtesy of Richard Avent).

Two cannon balls from a demi-culverin found inbedded in the masonry of the outer gatehouse of the castle (By courtesy of Richard Avent).

The badly damaged outer gatehouse of Laugharne Castle (in the foreground of this view) is more or less on line with the town's main street. It was probably parliamentary ordnance mounted in the now demolished north gate at the top of this street (where the alignment changes) which did so much damage to the gatehouse during the siege and bombardment (By courtesy of Richard Avent).

The southern side of the castle was well protected by its elevated position high above the Taf estuary and tidal marshes. But the north and north-east faces were far more vulnerable to bombardment from the rising ground north of the town. The ancient Glan y Mor earthwork on the far hill (top right) may have been used by the parliamentarians as a battery (By courtesy of Richard Avent).

Laugharne at the time of the Siege

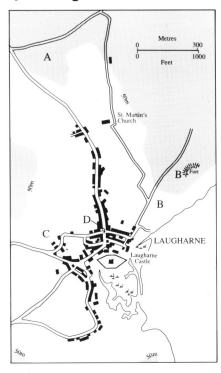

captured one of the town gatehouses (**D**), overwhelming the small isolated royalist force within. This may have been the north gate, located just 300 feet (85m) to the north of the castle's outer gatehouse. Ordnance mounted there enabled the parliamentarians to fire directly at the northern face of the outer gatehouse, and so into the gate-passage. A two-day bombardment, on 31 October and 1 November, eventually breached the gate — 'our guns played hard this day, and night, the next day also'. And, although attempts to set the gate on fire proved futile, Laugharne at length decided that the hole was large enough to risk a frontal assault on the castle.

Accordingly, at 11.00pm on Saturday evening, 2 November, following another day of heavy bombardment, the parliamentarians stormed both the damaged outer gatehouse and a defensive earthwork which stood in front of it. The royalists retreated back into the inner ward, but when Laugharne's men began to mine the walls they asked for a parley. Negotiations continued during the early hours of Sunday morning, terms were agreed, and at around 7.00am Laugharne took possession of the castle and of the arms, ammunition, ordnance and victuals within it. He had lost ten dead and 30 wounded; the royalists 33 dead and an unknown number of wounded. The rest of the king's men were allowed to march away, most of them to join the royalist garrison in Carmarthen.

Although Laugharne certainly garrisoned the castle for a time, it seems to have played little further part in the civil war. It was abandoned and slighted, either after the war or during spring 1645, when the garrison may have evacuated the place and rendered it untenable in the face of a renewed invasion of south-west Wales by Gerard's royalists.

The castle still bears the scars of its involvement in the war. The northern face of the outer gatehouse and its passage are badly damaged, probably the result of the bombardment of 31 October to 2 November. The damage to both the north-west tower at the entrance to the inner ward and the north-east tower may also have been caused by Laugharne's bombardment. The complete destruction of the north-east curtain wall of the outer ward and of the east wall of the inner ward is more likely to be the result of deliberate slighting, effected by gunpowder.

'Fierce and Doubtful Near an Hour':
The South-West

The familiar pattern of successive royalist and parliamentary waves rolling across Pembrokeshire was repeated once more in 1645. January 1645 marked a parliamentary high tide, with the newly-captured town and castle of Cardigan as high-water mark. Almost immediately, the royalists counter-attacked, sweeping into the town with over 2,000 men and besieging the castle. But Laugharne was able to send supplies to the garrison by boat and they held out until 22 January, when a force of around 350 parliamentarians approached. The royalists had broken down the bridge, but Laugharne managed to get his men across the river using 'faggots and other pieces of wood'. He then fell upon the royalists who, after a stiff street fight, were forced out of Cardigan and fell back on Newcastle Emlyn.

At the end of the winter, Gerard himself arrived back on the scene, marching across the heartlands of Wales, brushing aside parliamentary units at Llanidloes. In April, he swooped down on Laugharne's parliamentarians, who were besieging the royalist garrison of Newcastle Emlyn. The parliamentarians were surprised and outnumbered. Over 500 were killed or captured and the remainder fled west. Gerard lost no time in pursuing his enemies deep into Pembrokeshire, and the very next day he entered Haverfordwest unopposed, the parliamentarians hastily evacuating town and castle and pulling back into Pembroke and Tenby. Cardigan was now marooned, cut off by Gerard's men, but the parliamentary garrison were able to slip away by sea and join their colleagues in Pembroke.

With typical energy, Gerard turned upon minor bases in late April and early May. He stormed and took Picton Castle in a midnight attack, and secured Carew and other strongholds without serious resistance. But the royalists were unable to challenge parliament's hold on Tenby and Pembroke and by the end of May Gerard and most of his troops had disappeared, recalled to England. This time, they did not return. Instead, the tide turned finally in parliament's favour.

In April 1645, parliamentarians besieging Newcastle Emlyn were surprised by Gerard's royalists. As the parliamentary report put it, 'about six o'clock in the morning, there came a very strong party of the enemy's horse from England, besides other foot very numerous, who suddenly and secretly fell upon our men, slew and took most of our foot companies, besides many horse, [and] drove the rest into their garrisons'. The medieval castle did not finally fall to parliament until the end of the year. It was subsequently slighted.

Picton Castle changed hands twice during 1645, taken by Gerard in a night attack at the end of April and recaptured by parliament following a three-week siege in September. According to tradition, during Gerard's attack one of his officers dragged out a defender who had unwisely looked out of a ground-floor window. The incident was recorded in verse:

> 'By venturing only to trust
> His head a span beyond his post,
> By a general of the cavaliers
> Was dragged through a window by his ears'.

Although much altered and modernized, the core of the building at Picton dates from the end of the thirteenth century.

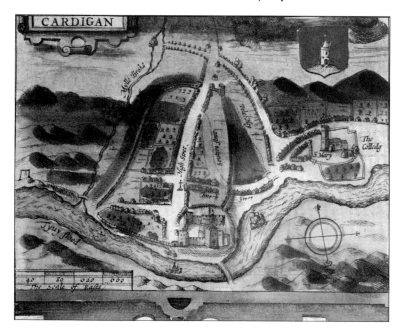

John Speed's map of early Stuart Cardigan. The town was completely dominated by the mighty medieval castle, which also controlled the only bridge over the lower reaches of the Teifi. In January 1645 the newly-captured town and castle was a parliamentary high-water mark. Almost immediately the royalists counter-attacked with over 2,000 men. Not until late January did Laugharne's parliamentarians force them out after a stiff street fight.

Colby Moor, fields and farmland still, was the scene of the royalist defeat of August 1645. For many decades thereafter, discarded arms and armour were regularly unearthed on the battlefield, and in the mid nineteenth century many bodies — thought to be civil war dead — were found in shallow, unmarked graves in nearby Wiston church. As late as the nineteenth century the phrase 'a Colby Moor rout' was common locally as a proverbial expression of chaos and confusion.

Laugharne spent several weeks rebuilding his army. By the end of July he was able to lead 1,000 men out of Pembroke in search of remaining royalist forces. In Haverfordwest Major Generals Stradling and Egerton rapidly assembled an army of 1,500 to meet them. The two forces clashed on Colby Moor, east of Haverfordwest, in the early evening of 1 August. Laugharne confessed that the engagement was 'very fierce and doubtful near an hour', but at length the royalist horse broke and fled and parliament was able to roll up the foot. Around 150 royalists were killed, and 700 more were captured. In the wake of this defeat, the remaining royalists abandoned the town of Haverfordwest, which Laugharne promptly secured, though they left a small garrison in the castle. A bombardment 'spent much ammunition to little purpose', but Laugharne's men succeeded in scaling the castle walls and firing the gatehouse. Carew and Manorbier were swiftly recovered, and the royalists at Picton surrendered on 20 September after a twenty-day siege. By the end of September the whole of Pembrokeshire was in parliament's hands.

Cardiganshire and Carmarthenshire then went the same way as much of south-east Wales. The counties declared for parliament during September, expelling most of the royalist troops still to be found there. The royalists had to abandon Cardigan and on 12 October Laugharne was welcomed into Carmarthen in triumph. There remained just two royalist bases to be cleared, both in Cardiganshire. A Colonel Lewes secured Newcastle Emlyn in December 1645 following a brief siege. To the north, Aberystwyth Castle put up greater resistance. It endured occasional attacks and sieges during the closing weeks of 1645 and a sustained investment from early 1646. Roger Whitley's royalist garrison finally surrendered to Rice Powell's besieging force on 14 April 1646.

'Starving is the only Way': The North-East

During the opening months of 1645 the king's men lost further ground in the northern Marches as Shrewsbury, Shropshire and most of Cheshire passed into parliament's hands, and as Chester itself became increasingly isolated. But at first parliament made little headway in north Wales. Holt and Wrexham changed hands several times, Hawarden was besieged, and Flintshire and Denbighshire

were repeatedly raided — houses were plundered and burnt almost indiscriminately, and even the home of the MP and leading parliamentarian, Sir John Trevor, was rifled. But attempts to establish further permanent bases in north-east Wales, or to push west into Merionethshire generally came to nothing. Parliament even lost control of Montgomery Castle briefly over the summer, for in May its governor, the flexible Sir John Price, a former royalist turned parliamentarian, returned to his old allegiance. In June, he turned again to parliament upon hearing of the king's defeat at Naseby.

In north Wales, the king's cause was effectively lost during autumn 1645. On 24 September many local troops fell at the battle of Rowton Moor, within sight of the now doomed city of Chester. Over the next few days Charles paid his last visit to Wales, gathering further troops in Denbighshire before marching off with them into England. Aware that the defences of the area were much depleted, he ordered Sir William Vaughan to gather reinforcements from remaining Marcher garrisons and bring them to north Wales. Vaughan obediently arrived in the area, and on 31 October mustered his troops on Denbigh Green, by Whitchurch. But local parliamentarians, aware of Vaughan's movements, gathered a force of around 2,500 men and swooped on the 2,000-strong royalist army at Denbigh Green on 1 November. Advancing from Ruthin, Mytton's parliamentarians first cleared the road of Vaughan's musketeers and then fell upon and broke his cavalry. Some of the royalist foot took refuge in nearby Denbigh Castle, but the horse were scattered and pursued for miles. The removal through death, capture, defeat or service elsewhere of so many royalists in autumn 1645 left north-east Wales open to invasion.

Accordingly, during the winter of 1645-46 Montgomeryshire was secured and most of Denbighshire and Flintshire quickly overrun by parliamentary troops who met almost no open resistance in the field. In the whole of north-east Wales there remained just a handful of isolated castles, each of which might have to be besieged. In fact, Chirk was quickly taken, surrendered in late February by Sir John Watts in return for a £200 bribe. With the king's permission Sir William Neale surrendered Hawarden in mid March. Ruthin proved more obdurate, enduring a six-week siege and bombardment. Only when

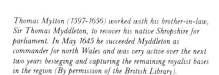

the parliamentary forces were so close that they were able to lay a mine beneath the walls did the garrison give up the uneven struggle. Mytton was much relieved when it surrendered on terms on 8 April.

Little information survives about the operations against Rhuddlan and Flint. Indeed, the role of these castles in the war as a whole is rather shadowy. We do know that Gilbert Byron's garrison in Rhuddlan were under siege by late May and surrendered on terms at the end of July. Flint Castle, too, was invested by late May and Colonel Roger Mostyn surrendered the place on 24 August. Mytton promised 'to use his best endeavours with the parliament on behalf of Colonel Mostyn, the Governor'.

In contrast, the siege of Denbigh is well documented, not least in the letters of its remarkable defender, William Salesbury. In April 1646 he politely but firmly declined Mytton's invitation to surrender, 'being loyall to my king... for the keeping of this place, His Majesty's own house, which (without regard to my own life, lands or posterity) with God's assistance, I will endeavour to make good for him to my last gasp. Soe I rest your poor kinsman and old play fellow'. There followed a long formal siege, the parliamentarians making Whitchurch their first headquarters and using the church tower as a lookout. The parliamentary bombardment was directed particularly at the Goblin Tower, thought to contain the only reliable well. But the mighty walls and towers held firm, and so did Salesbury and his 500 strong garrison. Not until he received written permission from the king did Salesbury contemplate surrender. Terms were agreed in mid October and the castle was handed over on the 26th. Salesbury told Mytton, 'if I must quit this place, I confesse I had rather you had the honour of it than any other person in England of your party'.

The last castle to hold out for the king in north-east Wales appeared far less formidable. Holt bridge had been secured for parliament by the end of 1645, but a small royalist garrison under Sir Richard Lloyd held out in the medieval castle. It was, the parliamentarians noted, 'a very strong place. Starving is the only way that we can use against that place'. Holt was under siege or blockade for most of 1646, the parliamentary forces harassed by frequent counter-attacks from Lloyd's men. Finally, on 13 January 1647, Holt Castle was surrendered on terms.

The hill-top at Denbigh was fortified by Henry de Lacy for King Edward I at the end of the thirteenth century, with a castle and a circuit of town walls connected to it (below). By the fifteenth century, most people had quit this high, cramped enclosure and the main town grew up on lower ground beneath the castle to the north. The town soon fell to Mytton in 1646, but the hill-top enclosure — both the castle proper and the walled but largely deserted site of the old town, now in effect the outer ward of the castle — held out for many months under William Salesbury. Parliamentary guns were trained upon the Goblin Tower (above), the basement of which contained a vital water supply. But neither water nor courage failed, and the royalists held out for months until they received permission from the king to surrender on terms.

The bridge at Llanrwst, known as Pont Fawr, was a vital crossing of the River Conwy. Curiously, the royalists failed to fortify this bridge in 1646 and Thomas Mytton was able to enter Caernarvonshire without resistance and to by-pass Conwy itself (By courtesy of the National Monuments Record, Wales).

'The Governor ... Delivered the Keys': The North-West

The north-western counties escaped direct military involvement in the war until spring 1646. On 24 April Mytton and his men entered Caernarvonshire, crossing Llanrwst bridge, which the royalists had neglected to defend or to break down. By-passing Conwy, they marched straight to the walled town of Caernarfon. Mytton's men met no resistance in the field, for at their appearance, most of the county's gentry promptly declared for parliament. As Archbishop Williams put it in late April, 'what they will say in the end of the day I do not know, nor do I care, if I could with mine own sacrificing keep this poor country from being ruined'. But Lord Byron and his garrison were determined to hang on to Caernarfon for as long as possible, still pinning their hopes on reinforcements from Ireland. Besieged and bombarded by land and sea, the town fell to parliament in May. Convinced at last of the hopelessness of their position, Byron and his men surrendered the castle on 4 June. The terms included free quarter for a bear and his keeper who had entertained the garrison.

Mytton was then free to turn his attention to the only other royalist base in Caernarvonshire — Conwy. On 8 August the walled town was attacked, some of the troops creating a diversion by the north wall while the main force scaled the south and west walls. The tactic worked and, even though the scaling ladders proved too short, the walls were carried and the town taken. Many 'Irish' prisoners were tied back to back, taken out to sea and 'sent by water to their own country'. Owen held out in the castle, scornfully refusing Mytton's summons to surrender. It took a further three months of close siege and heavy bombardment before Owen gave up the struggle. Conwy Castle surrendered on terms on 18 November.

While the Caernarvonshire strongholds were still being reduced, the whole of Anglesey had submitted to parliament without a shot being fired. During April and May Captain Rich in the *Rebecca* anchored off Beaumaris and made contact with the local gentry. Initial discussions seemed promising and Mytton appointed commissioners to conduct formal negotiations. On 14 June a treaty was concluded and the whole of Anglesey, including Beaumaris Castle, its only major stronghold, was surrendered to parliament.

After the fall of Conwy castle in November, only one fortress remained for the king in north-west Wales. Harlech Castle in Merionethshire was remote and inaccessible to men and cannon alike. Garrisoned by William Owen since spring 1644, Harlech seems to have been under siege by late June 1646. The town fell, but the castle held out, even when the number of active soldiers in the garrison fell to just 28. They were divided into two watches in order to defend the place night and day. Articles of surrender were finally agreed on 15 March 1647. On 'the 16th day, being Tuesday, the Governor, Mr William Owen, delivered the keys of the castle to General Mytton'. The civil war in Wales was over.

Above Left: *The Edwardian fortress at Harlech, built in 1283-89 had been well maintained during the sixteenth and early seventeenth centuries, not least because assize judges lodged there when on circuit.*
Left: *From spring 1644 Harlech was garrisoned for the king by William Owen (1607-70), younger brother of Sir John Owen. When the garrison eventually surrendered on terms to the besieging force in March 1647 — the last mainland base to do so — there were within the castle sixteen officers, gentlemen and invalids and just 28 active soldiers (By courtesy of the National Library of Wales).*

Principal Areas of
Royalist Activity

Advance of the
Royalist Scottish Army

PRESTON
[August 1648]

Renewed Fighting

Although military conflict ended in 1646, political settlement was elusive. The defeated, captive king conducted long and futile negotiations with parliament. To make matters worse, there were growing divisions between parliament and its army, in part over the direction of the proposed political and religious settlement, in part over mundane issues such as paying army arrears, providing for soldiers' widows and orphans, and granting indemnity for wartime actions. The army seized the initiative by abducting Charles and negotiating with him direct.

The futile negotiations and the growing rifts, both between parliament and its army and within the army itself, were cut short by Charles's flight to the Isle of Wight at the end of 1647 and his treaty with the Scots. As a result, a Scottish royalist army invaded England in summer 1648; it was crushed by Cromwell at Preston. Throughout 1648 there were also poorly co-ordinated royalist rebellions in various parts of England and Wales, all in due course put down by the parliamentary army. The renewed sporadic violence of 1648 is sometimes called 'the second civil war'. In its wake, conservative elements in parliament were purged by the army and the king was tried and executed.

Many Welshmen retained deep loyalty to their king and took up arms again in 1648, hoping that their actions would form part of a wider rebellion which would lead to the defeat of the parliamentarians. Although the royalists had been treated leniently after 1646, parliamentary control remained unpalatable or obnoxious to many. The new parliamentary county administrations imposed heavy taxes and new religious practices, and were supported by garrisons of English troops under English governors. To make matters worse, after 1646 there was a proliferation of local disputes between men who claimed to have supported parliament from the outset and those who only came over to parliament towards the end of the war. Genuine pro-royalist sentiments, localist opposition to 'foreign' or burdensome administrations, and squabbles between different groups now carrying parliamentary labels all lie behind the renewed violence in Wales in 1648.

Royal Armouries XII.1638

Arms and Armour of the Civil War: Infantry 2

Civil war musketeers generally wore no armour. They were not defenceless, for they had swords and could use their muskets as clubs. But they relied heavily upon their gunfire and the pikemen to keep their opponents at a safe distance. The wheellock mechanism was not employed in civil war muskets, which instead were either flintlocks or matchlocks (shown here). In the latter, a slow burning matchcord was used to ignite the charge. Wind and rain might put the match out, and a moment's carelessness could ignite the gunpowder held about the musketeer's person — with lethal consequences. With their four-foot (1.2m) barrels, muskets had a far greater range than either pistols or carbines and were more accurate, though accuracy was not a strongpoint of seventeenth-century firearms. To be effective, therefore, musketeers deployed in blocks, each rank successively firing a volley of shots into the enemy (By courtesy of the Board of Trustees of the Royal Armouries).

'A Spiteful, Mischievous People': Rebellion in the South

Pembroke had been loyal to parliament throughout the civil war and, for much of it, had been parliament's only base in Wales. Yet in 1648 this same town was a centre of rebellion. Trouble initially flared in the opening weeks of 1648 when parliament sent Colonel Fleming to take command of Pembroke castle and to oversee the disbanding of local troops. The incumbent governor, John Poyer, refused to co-operate. He had been loyal to parliament throughout the civil war, yet after 1646 he had seen county government placed in the hands of local families like the Lorts, who had been active royalists for much of the war and had only come over to parliament in its closing stages. Poyer and his old colleagues, Rowland Laugharne and Rice Powell, were enraged to see trimmers and ex-royalists in power and feared that local disputes over property, money and war-time accounts would be decided against them by the Lort clique. These tensions and fears erupted when Fleming arrived to relieve Poyer of his command and to take control of the county's powerbase.

Ever more desperate, in mid March Poyer openly declared for the king. Fleming and his men were driven out of Pembroke and discontented troops flooded into the town. Colonel Reade and 350 parliamentary troops were sent from Bristol to restore order. They landed at Pwllcrochan on 28 March, but on the following day were surprised and overwhelmed by Poyer's men as they quartered in and around St Mary's church. They were subsequently disarmed and allowed to march out of the region. Fleming and other officers rapidly fled from nearby Henllan. Growing ever stronger, the rebels took control of Tenby and Carmarthen. A parliamentary pamphlet bitterly attacked the acquiescent attitude of the locals, 'a spiteful, mischievous people... these little less than barbarous people'. It went on, somewhat questionably in the light of recent events, to allege that, 'the Welsh have always been observed to be cowards and seldom act but upon advantage'.

St Mary's Church, Pwllcrochan, the scene of the one-sided engagement of March 1648. Two companies of troops, sent by water from Bristol to restore order in south-west Wales, were using the church as overnight accommodation when they were surprised by a large body of rebels. Despite fierce resistance, the parliamentarians were forced to surrender on terms and were then allowed to march off to Cardiff.

Pembroke Castle had been held by parliament throughout the civil war, often its only secure base within Wales. But in 1648 the castle and adjoining walled town became the centre of royalist rebellion, one of whose leaders was the very officer who had held Pembroke so heroically against the king's men.

For the moment, the advantage seemed to lie with the royalist rebels. Colonel Reade's men having failed to quell the rebellion, Colonel Horton led his parliamentary troops from Brecon to attempt to crush it. To hinder their advance, Poyer broke down the bridges spanning the lower reaches of the Tywi. Dispatched by Horton to try and seize a pass, Fleming and his men were lured into a rebel ambush. They sought refuge in Llandeilo church but the rebels pushed home their attack, taking over 100 prisoners. Fleming was found dead in the church. Horton retired eastwards, allowing the rebels to enter Glamorgan. With Laugharne and Powell now apparently in command, the rebel army took Swansea and Neath in early May and pressed on eastwards, doubtless intending to secure Cardiff. But before they reached that town, Horton intervened again.

Battle of St Fagan's, May 1648

Through the pouring rain of early May, Horton marched south from Brecon and arrived at St Fagan's on the 4th. He posted men at key crossings of the rivers Taff and Ely, but he kept the bulk of his force around St Fagan's, clearly hoping to block the rebel advance on Cardiff. In fact, the rebel army was already within two miles (3.2km) of St Fagan's, and there was some minor skirmishing as scouting and foraging parties clashed. But no major engagement followed and the main rebel force halted at St Nicholas. The pattern was repeated on the following day, with the opposing armies, barely two miles (3.2km) from each other, indulging in minor skirmishes and raids, but holding back from full-scale engagement. On 6 May, the rebels pulled back to the Llancarfan-Penmark area to regroup and consider their options. Horten kept his main force stationed in and to the north of St Fagan's.

With Horton so near Cardiff, the rebels stood no chance of avoiding the parliamentary army and seizing the town unhindered. They could, of course, simply retreat westwards and seek to make a stand on more favourable ground. It might have been to their advantage to avoid a formal battle with Horton, and instead resort to 'guerilla' tactics, dividing into raiding parties and repeatedly attacking Horton's quarters and other parliamentary units and garrisons. However, news reached them that Oliver Cromwell had already left London with part of the parliamentary army and was advancing on south Wales to crush the rebellion. The rebel army, now under the overall command of Laugharne, decided that their only chance of success was to engage Horton's men in battle, and to do so before Cromwell arrived.

Thus, on the night of 7-8 May, the rebels marched back to St Nicholas and beyond, crossing the Ely near Peterston, moving through St Bride's, and approaching St Fagan's from the west. Their army numbered roughly 8,000, most of them inexperienced and poorly armed infantry; Laugharne had very few horse. They deployed north — south along the valley of the Nant Dowlais, and probably on the western side of that stream. Half a mile (0.8km) to the east, Horton had deployed his 3,000 well-equipped parliamentary veterans in a mile-long (1.6km) front on rising ground north-west of St Fagan's. The infantry were placed in the centre, with cavalry on each wing. Both armies spanned the minor road which ran (and still runs) from St Bride's to Fairwater, though the bulk of both forces lay north of this road.

It is difficult now to reconstruct the battle of St Fagan's. The terrain has been altered by the laying and removal of two railway lines, with associated cuttings and embankments, the draining of marshland, the diverting or culverting of streams, and so on. In addition, contemporary accounts of the battle are few in number, vague or ambiguous in content and parliamentarian in origin; no rebel account of the action seems to have survived.

The battle was fought in the early morning of 8 May, the two armies clashing on the wet, muddy ground, enclosed by hedges and fences, a mile (1.6km) or more to the north-west of St Fagan's. The village itself was left unoccupied by the parliamentarians, and early in the day a unit of rebel horse, under Colonel Butler, moved forward and entered it unopposed. In theory, Horton was now under threat from both sides, but, in practice, Butler's horse seem to have played no significant part in the ensuing action. Battle proper began with the advance units — 'forlorn hopes' — of both armies moving forward and clashing in the centre of the field. A more general advance quickly followed.

The battlefield of St Fagan's. In his report to parliament after the battle, Colonel Horton stressed the dangers his men faced, penned in between the mountains and the sea, between a numerically superior enemy to the west and the uncertainties of Chepstow and Monmouthshire to the east. But God had delivered them, wrote Horton: 'That God should please in this condition so to own us, as to make a way for us through the midst of our enemies and to scatter them every way, is a mercy not to be forgotten, especially by those who have more immediately tasted of it'.

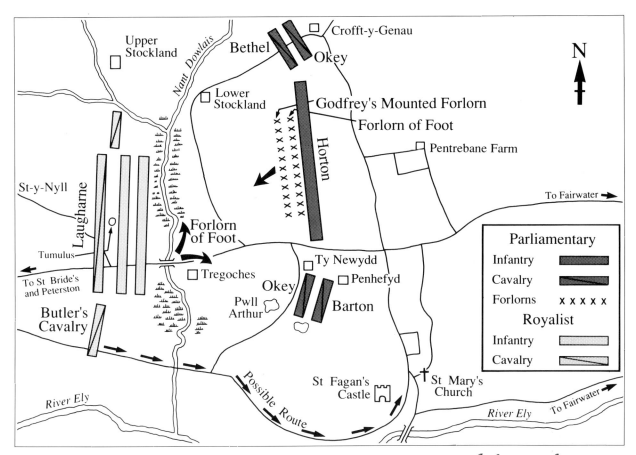

A Possible Reconstruction of the Battle

Colonel John Okey rose from humble origins to be one of the senior commanders of the parliamentary army. He played a leading role in most of the key engagements of the closing years of the civil war, and in spring 1648 he assisted Horton at St Fagan's. Okey's specialism was as commander of dragoons, that is mounted troops who rode forward to advanced positions and might fight on horseback, but who usually then dismounted and fought on foot. They were used to clear the enemy from hedges and ditches or to provide flanking fire. Okey's dragoons did good service at St Fagan's, helping the regular cavalry to dislodge rebels from hedged enclosures and to push them over the brook.

The engagement soon developed into a dour struggle in which the better equipped and more experienced parliamentarians slowly pushed back their numerically superior opponents. The parliamentary advantage in horse was particularly telling, for time and again cavalry charges dislodged the rebels and allowed the parliamentary infantry to move forward and consolidate the territorial gains. The rebels were thrown back over the Nant Dowlais, and although they made a determined effort to hold the bridge where the St Bride's to Fairwater road crossed the stream, they found themselves under increasing pressure. Eventually, after a two-hour fight, the rebel foot broke and fled west. They may have tried to make a stand at a second bridge, presumably one of those spanning the Ely, but to no avail. The parliamentarians pursued their broken enemies for several miles.

Horton claimed to have lost very few men. Perhaps some 150 to 200 rebels perished at St Fagan's, and later stories that the Ely flowed red with blood may owe much to poetic licence. But over 3,000 men rebels were captured and many more were scattered or deserted in the wake of the defeat. Powell, Poyer and the wounded Laugharne were able to lead very few men back to Pembrokeshire.

Left: *Although Oliver Cromwell had played no part in the civil war in Wales in 1642-47, in 1648 he was sent to south Wales to put down the rebellion. This miniature, dating from 1656, is by Samuel Cooper (By courtesy of the National Portrait Gallery).*

Below: *Cromwell swiftly retook Chepstow town but, when the castle continued to resist, he and his main force moved on. Colonel Ewer, left behind to besiege and bombard the place into submission, deployed heavy guns brought from Gloucester and Bristol. At length, part of the outer wall on the landward side was breached.*

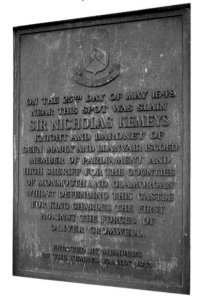

The modern memorial to Sir Nicholas Kemeys in Chepstow Castle. Sir Nicholas, created a baronet by the king in 1642, was an active royalist throughout the war, and in 1648 he became leader of the rebels who seized the medieval stronghold at Chepstow. Even when heavily outnumbered by parliamentary troops and with the castle wall breached, he still tried to hold out. Kemeys and a few of his fellow rebels perished when Ewer's men stormed the fortress.

To add to royalist gloom, Cromwell's large parliamentary army, sent from London to crush the rebellion, entered Wales in the second week of May. Sir Nicholas Kemeys had seized Chepstow in the king's name and had established a strong garrison in the castle. On 11 May Cromwell retook the town, forcing the town gate and overwhelming the defenders. The castle, however, held out. On 14 May Cromwell and the main force moved on, leaving troops under Colonel Ewer to continue the operation. After a heavy bombardment, parts of the castle wall were breached. When the garrison refused to surrender unconditionally, Ewer stormed the place on 25 May, killing some of the rebels, including Kemeys, and taking over 100 prisoners.

Moving swiftly west through the now cleared counties of Glamorgan and Carmarthenshire, Cromwell arrived in south Pembrokeshire on 24 May. Only two towns remained in rebel hands. Tenby, already under siege by Colonel Horton, surrendered on 31 May, giving parliament a rich haul of prisoners — including Rice Powell — arms, and ammunition. Cromwell sat down before Pembroke, intending to starve or bombard the walled town and its mighty medieval castle into submission. At first Cromwell possessed only light guns, ineffective against the thick masonry walls. Attempts to take the town by storm during June were repulsed with losses. Eventually, heavy guns arrived by sea, and in early July the walls were breached in several places. Within Pembroke food and other supplies were also running very short. Town and castle were finally surrendered on 11 July and the leaders of the rebellion, Poyer and Laugharne, joined Powell in a parliamentary prison to await trial. The rebellion in south Wales was over.

'Quell or Appease the Insurrection': Trouble in the North-West

Most of north Wales remained loyal to parliament in 1648. Only two areas saw serious bloodshed, and those disturbances were quite separate and took place at different times. In May and early June, Sir John Owen led an abortive revolt in Caernarvonshire; in the late summer there was a shortlived rebellion on Anglesey. The trouble in north Wales was less serious than that in the south and it was left to local commanders to crush it.

Armed with a commission issued in Charles's name, the local royalist leader, Sir John Owen, tried to raise north-west Wales for the king in May 1648. A local parliamentary officer, Colonel John Carter, wrote hurriedly that the gentry were making no effort to 'quell or appease the insurrection' and instead were giving it moral or actual support in the hope of removing parliamentary garrisons from the area. In fact, Owen met with a cool response in Merionethshire but in Caernarvonshire he gathered scores of armed men. With these, he raided parliamentary garrisons, and by the beginning of June Major-General Mytton in Caernarfon found himself virtually besieged.

Relief, however, was soon at hand. During late May a parliamentary force under Colonel George Twistleton, governor of Denbigh, had been active in north-west Wales, rounding up rebel bands and searching in vain for Owen's main force. Summoned to Caernarfon by Mytton, on 5 June Twistleton and Carter found their route blocked by Owen on the coast road between Penrhyn and Aber.

The castle and walled town of Caernarfon. By the beginning of June 1648 the rebellion on the mainland had reached such proportions that Mytton and his parliamentary garrison were virtually besieged within Edward I's great stronghold.

Owen's 250 troops clashed with the 200-strong parliamentary force at a spot known as Y Dalar Hir. The running fight ended with over 60 rebels, including Owen, captured, and the remainder fleeing in disorder. The Caernarvonshire rebellion was over. Owen was held for a time in Denbigh castle, where an unsuccessful attempt was made to rescue him.

In July 1648 Anglesey declared for the king. Lord Byron had arrived on the island, bearing news of the Scottish invasion and other royalist risings. His arrival successfully triggered rebellion, the leading gentry of the island signing and issuing a royalist manifesto. But Byron's hopes of leading the rebellion were dashed when the gentry instead chose a local man, Richard Bulkeley of Baron Hill, as their leader. During July many disaffected royalists from the Welsh mainland crossed the Menai Strait to join the rebellion.

The parliamentarians were well aware of these developments. Mytton and Myddleton, comrades in arms once more, gathered 1,500 men around Bangor. A small fleet of ships, assembled in Conwy, picked them up and carried them across to Anglesey at the end of September. They landed at dusk at Cadnant creek and, overcoming surprisingly light resistance, regrouped and marched towards the rebel stronghold of Beaumaris. The royalists came out to meet them and took up position on Red Hill, a mile (1.6km) or so west of the town. The two armies clashed on the afternoon of 1 October. Although the casualties were fairly even — around 30 to 40 dead on each side — the rebels were no match for the well-armed and well-organized professionals. The royalists broke and fled, over 400 of them falling prisoner and the rest scrambling back into Beaumaris Castle. The town was taken without resistance and the castle was surrendered on the following day when the parliamentary commanders threatened to hang their prisoners. Order had been restored.

The 1648 Rebellion in North-West Wales

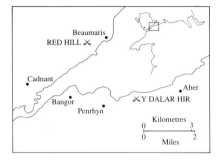

Beaumaris Castle from the north, with the Menai Strait and the mountains of Caernarvonshire in the background. 'Utterlie decayed' in 1609, the castle had subsequently been repaired and refortified by the Bulkeley family and during the civil war it was a vital staging post for men and supplies coming from Ireland to aid the royalist cause in England and Wales. After the war, the castle was maintained and garrisoned by parliament for several years. It was slighted during the late 1650s and 1660s.

Chapter 8

Aftermath and Impact

Punishment

The inner porch at Beaupre, home of the Bassett family of Glamorgan. Their crest and motto appear on the porch, which was built in 1600. Sir Richard Bassett was royalist sheriff of Glamorgan, governor of Cardiff for a few months during 1645, and one of the leading rebels of 1648. He was heavily fined by parliament, spent several years abroad and may have partially abandoned Beaupre in favour of a smaller, cheaper residence. The house remained in the family for a time, but the Bassetts were struggling against debts incurred in the war and were finally forced to sell Beaupre in 1709.

In Wales, as in England, the defeated royalists had been treated very leniently after 1646. The common soldiers were allowed to return home unhindered, and their officers and the king's civilian administrators usually escaped with modest fines. The marquis of Worcester was one of very few to suffer imprisonment, though death (from natural causes) soon released him and he was given an honourable burial at Windsor. But after the 1648 rebellion parliament and its army officers adopted a firmer line, both because the rebels had needlessly reopened the conflict and because so many of them had held military or civilian office under parliament and had, therefore, betrayed their trust. Again, most of the rank and file were simply disarmed and allowed home on swearing an oath 'never to engage against the parliament hereafter', though Horton arranged for 240 bachelors taken at St Fagan's to be shipped to 'the Barbadoes'. In contrast, the military leaders of the rebellion and their gentry supporters suffered more general repression.

Of the ringleaders, Kemeys had perished at Chepstow and at least four officers captured at St Fagan's were swiftly courtmartialled, sentenced to death and executed, three of them shot, the other hanged. The three leading lights of the Pembrokeshire uprising — Poyer, Powell and Laugharne — were taken to London, tried and condemned to death. In the end only Poyer was executed, shot by firing squad in Covent Garden. Sir John Owen, leader of the Caernarvonshire rebellion, was also tried and condemned in London, though he too was reprieved. Richard Bulkeley of Anglesey went into exile on the Continent after the collapse of the rebellion, but he was back home by the following year. Soon after, a chance encounter with Major Richard Cheadle on the shores of the Menai Strait saw the old Bulkeley-Cheadle feud erupt once more. A duel left Bulkeley dead and Cheadle was subsequently arrested and hanged at Conwy beach.

Widespread financial retribution followed the rebellion. A general fine of £16,000 was imposed upon north Wales, the bulk of it to be paid by Anglesey and Caernarvonshire, the two counties in the forefront of the rebellion. Throughout Wales, individual royalists who had been prominent in the civil war or the 1648 rebellion were held to account and found their property in danger. A few had their estates confiscated or were forced to sell up to pay fines and other debts incurred during the conflict. Most compounded for their delinquency, that is, paid a 'composition' fine based upon the capital value of their estates and took an oath of loyalty to parliament. In return, their estates would be restored or the threat of confiscation lifted and their political records indemnified. County committees were established to deal with sequestration and compounding, though final decisions rested with London-based bodies. Fines ranged from less than £50 to well over £1,000 depending upon the seriousness of the 'crimes' and the value of the estate. The surviving evidence is incomplete and no definitive totals can be reached, but it appears that composition fines were paid on over 100 estates in Wales and Monmouthshire.

Castles at War III: Destruction

Few, if any, Welsh castles were completely wrecked by bombardment or mining in the course of enemy sieges. Most survived the war largely unscathed. Instead, it was the subsequent actions of parliament which caused so much destruction and altered the face of Wales. In order to punish their usually pro-royalist owners and to guard against further trouble, directions were given that the fortifications be deliberately damaged or 'slighted' in order to render them useless for military action.

In 1646-47, when the main war was over, parliament ordered quite modest demolitions, often merely the levelling of banks, ditches and other earthworks which had been thrown up around many castles during the civil war. This may explain why so few civil war earthworks survive today. But in the wake of the renewed rebellion of 1648, parliament went much further and ordered the extensive demolition of many of the castles themselves.

Not all Welsh castles involved in the war were slighted. A few, such as Chepstow, and Ludlow on the borders, were hastily repaired and continued in use as prisons and administrative centres. Some — Caernarfon and Harlech, for example — which had survived the war largely intact seem to have escaped demolition. At Beaumaris, Conwy and Denbigh major demolition occurred later, after the restoration, when the redundant buildings were stripped of reusable materials. But most civil war strongholds were deliberately slighted on parliament's orders during the period 1648-50.

Slighting was often a complex and lengthy business, with several dozen men employed for months on end. Some particularly detailed accounts survive for the demolition of Montgomery Castle between June and October 1649, showing that up to 150 general labourers were employed on the site, as well as smaller numbers of specialist carpenters, masons and miners. Wages and other costs totalled around £675. But at Montgomery, as elsewhere, slighting could be profitable, for anything valuable or reusable was carefully removed prior to demolition. The lead and tiles from the roofs, the glass from the windows, the stone fireplaces, and any panelling and good quality boards and timbers were stripped out and resold.

The slighted and shattered remains of Montgomery Castle, as engraved by Samuel and Nathaniel Buck during the 1740s. The Bucks did a 'roaring trade' in slightly romanticized engravings of ruined houses, abbeys and castles.

Above: *A possible reconstruction of the early stages of the post-war slighting of Raglan Castle, with battlements and upper levels of the keep being demolished with hand tools. In due course, rather more drastic methods were employed, and one side of the keep was brought down by undermining or with gunpowder. The moat around the keep, together with the castle fishponds, were drained in vain search for plate, coin or other treasure (Illustration by Roger Jones).*

Left: *Flint Castle was the first of the string of mighty fortresses which Edward I built in north Wales. It had an uneventful civil war, surrendering to Mytton in August 1646 after a lengthy but poorly documented siege. For a time, it was garrisoned for parliament and one tower was used as a prison, but in 1647 the place was disgarrisoned and extensively slighted, probably using explosives.*

Some castles, including Flint, Laugharne, Pembroke, Raglan and Rhuddlan, were rendered untenable by demolishing a section of the curtain wall or perhaps one side of the keep. The workmen either had the laborious task of knocking down the masonry with picks and crowbars, or set and sprang mines beneath the chosen wall. At Haverfordwest, the townsmen found it impossible to make any impression using hand tools and appealed to Cromwell for some gunpowder to help them bring down part of the castle. Other once strong medieval fortresses, such as Abergavenny, Aberystwyth, Montgomery and Ruthin, were completely wrecked, probably by quite extensive use of explosives. By 1700 only a handful of castles in Wales could be considered habitable and in good order. Most had already become shattered and picturesque ruins.

Local Government

Inevitably, the personnel of local government also changed after the civil war and again after the 1648 rebellion, as prominent royalists were weeded out and parliamentarians took their place. In most counties some of the notionally royalist administrators of the early and mid 1640s had been sufficiently tactful during the years of royal dominance and had declared for parliament sufficiently swiftly and vehemently in 1645-46 to be acceptable to parliament and to be retained after the civil war. In those counties which avoided further trouble, many pre-1646 politicians held office to the restoration and beyond, so providing a degree of stability and continuity. Again, it was the 1648 rebellion which cut deep. In its wake, many of the existing local politicians in Glamorgan and Pembrokeshire promptly lost office. A similar purge in Anglesey left so few local gentry considered trustworthy that the island was placed under non-local, semi-military government.

Anglesey apart, the prominent royalists removed from county government in 1646 or 1648 were usually replaced by other local gentry — albeit perhaps members of the lesser rather than the greater gentry. For all the military and political disruptions of the war years, there was no great social upheaval and the old gentry elite survived largely intact. Most gentry families were able to weather the storm, to meet their composition fines and other exactions and to retain their social position. Accordingly, even if the political fortunes of some waned a little during the 1650s, almost all survived socially and economically to come into their own again after 1660. Detailed county studies suggest that most gentry families of 1640 retained their position in 1660 or had recovered it long before 1700. In Glamorgan, for example, civil war losses undoubtedly contributed to the debts which later ruined the Stradlings, the Bassetts and the Thomases. But almost all the gentry families of 1600 were still politically and socially dominant in 1700.

New Men

In Glamorgan and elsewhere this remarkably durable elite did find their ranks swollen by some new men. The upheavals of the mid seventeenth century may have been marked, not so much by the destruction of old families, as by the arrival of some new. The most spectacular *arriviste* in Wales was Philip Jones. Born of humble Glamorgan stock and worth perhaps £20 per year in 1640, he rose rapidly in parliament's service during the civil war, played an important role in central government during the interregnum, and, for much of the 1650s, was the dominant force in south Walian politics. In barely twenty years Jones amassed a huge fortune, most of which he retained at the restoration, and he went on to cement his position amongst the Glamorgan elite, and to establish a dynasty lasting several generations.

If the magnitude of Jones's success was unrivalled in Wales, the route he followed was far from unique. Colonel John Carter, son of a Buckinghamshire linen draper, was parliament's commander-in-chief in north Wales during the 1650s. He used his position to mop up important offices — high sheriff, lord lieutenant, MP — and to acquire wealth, both through his own activities, and through his marriage to a Denbighshire heiress. A well-timed transfer of allegiance ensured that he survived the restoration unmolested and went on to gain further money and offices during the 1660s. He was

No-one in Wales gained more from the civil war than Philip Jones (bottom). He played little part in the actual fighting, but during the 1650s he monopolized local office and dominated all the influential county committees. As a Protectoral councillor and close friend of Cromwell, he was also one of the most powerful figures in central government. As one contemporary put it, 'he made hay while the sun shined', and amassed a huge fortune. With it, he acquired Fonmon Castle (top), a medieval mansion in the Vale of Glamorgan. It was extended in the late seventeenth century and remodelled in the eighteenth. Jones survived the restoration largely unscathed and retained both Fonmon and most of his fortune (By courtesy of Sir Brooke Boothby).

The monument to Archbishop Williams in Llandygai church. He had a colourful career, veering between royal favour and disfavour. A royalist for much of the war, in 1645 he was unceremoniously dumped from Conwy Castle by fellow royalist Sir John Owen. In the following year, he assisted parliament in the conquest of north-west Wales. The archbishop died in 1650 (By courtesy of the National Monuments Record, Wales).

John Robinson's monument in Gresford church. An active royalist throughout the war, he saw action at Holt, Hawarden, Chester and Caernarfon. Following a period in exile during the 1650s, he returned to north Wales and to office after the restoration. The Latin inscription closes: 'His body, though formed of superior clay, yet being worn out as well as ennobled by honourable wounds, was unable to retain beyond the 65th year of his age his soul, which aspired to heaven, and surrendered it on 15 March 1680 of the Christian era' (By courtesy of the Conway Library, Courtauld Institute of Art).

knighted both by Protector Cromwell and by Charles II. Carter's comrade in arms at Y Dalar Hir, Colonel George Twistleton, also married a north Wales heiress and settled down to a life of unaccustomed affluence.

Old Soldiers

Jones, Carter, Twistleton and others etablished themselves and joined the ranks of the political and social elite. Not all the commanders active in Wales during the war fared so well. Arthur, Lord Capel, was executed for his part in the 1648 rebellion, and during the 1650s death in battle or in bed removed many other senior figures — Lord Byron, Sir William Vavasour, Sir Jacob Astley, Prince Maurice, Archbishop John Williams, Thomas Mytton, Thomas Horton and others. William Salesbury followed them in 1660. A few survived to gain rewards and offices under Charles II. Rowland Laugharne became an MP; Sir John Owen and John Robinson were successively vice-admiral of north Wales; Sir John Mennes became a naval administrator; Charles Gerard resumed a stormy career which saw him created first earl of Macclesfield; and Roger Mostyn, who had spent or lost over £60,000 in the king's cause, and the eldest son of Sir Thomas Myddleton, who had declared for Charles II in 1659, were both created baronets. The king proposed creating a completely new honour, the Order of the Royal Oak, for individual gentry (or their heirs) who had been particularly prominent in his father's cause during the 1640s. Seventy-five members of the Welsh and Monmouthshire gentry were nominated. In the end the idea was scrapped.

Provision was also made after the restoration to help maimed or indigent ex-soldiers who had suffered in the king's army during the civil war. Application for financial relief was to be made to the local JPs, and their records give us a glimpse of the impact of war at a lower level of society. The Caernarvonshire records, for example, contain a litany of woe: 'Robert Owen of Caerhun, maymed of the hand and wounded on the head in Nasbie fight, a very poor man; Roland Owen of Clynog, hurt and made a cripple; David Owen of Conwy, shott under the eye very dangerously and the bullet remaineth under the ear, and have several wounds; William Morris of Llanarmon, quite maymed and hath lost his right hand being shott with a Canon bullet; William Griffith of Llanllechid, aged 87, an old soldier to Queen Elizabeth, King James and the late king, hath several wounds and lost two sons in the king's service; Symon ap William Lewis of Llanbeblig, shott under the eare and out at the chop, and also in the shoulder whereof he still languisheth'.

The Impact of the War

There is now no way of telling how many Welshmen fought in the civil war, nor how many were killed or wounded. Perhaps the best clue comes from the account which Richard Gough wrote of his life in Myddle, Shropshire. From Myddle and two neighbouring villages twenty men went off to fight for the king, of whom thirteen either perished or never returned, presumed killed. Two of them were 'cut in pieces' when Hopton Castle fell and a third, bedridden in Bridgnorth following an alehouse fight with fellow royalists, was burnt to death 'being unable to help himself' when the parliamentarians attacked the town. In addition, several local men fought for parliament, one of whom returned maimed, his femur broken by musket shot and his leg 'very crooked as long as he lived'. As Gough concluded, 'if so many died out of these three towns, we may reasonably guess that many thousands died in England in that war'. Wales, too, must have lost many a son.

Although much of Wales escaped serious fighting and bloodshed, the effects of war hit everyone. Recruitment and impressment removed a significant proportion of the male population throughout the country. County commissioners doubtless exaggerated, but there may have been a basis of truth in reports like that from west Glamorgan in 1644: 'these parts are so gleaned of all spare people... that the husbandmen will be hardly able to manage their tillage. And thereby not only a scarcity of grain will ensue but also an inability to maintain any necessary charge'. On top of the temporary or permanent removal of the strongest members of the community, every town, village or rural parish suffered repeated and heavy financial demands as king and parliament imposed old and new taxes in an attempt to maintain the war effort. To the same ends, horses were confiscated, cavalry units grazed on any available field or crop, and foraging parties of armed troops appeared to seize provisions. The Welsh sea-borne trade was severely disrupted and overland commerce with England, particularly the crucial cattle trade, was all but halted. No-one in Wales, not even in darkest, peaceful Merionethshire or Breconshire, could have been unaware of, and unaffected by, the civil war.

Some, of course, would have felt the impact of war more directly — those living within a walled town or close to a defendable castle, the inhabitants of southern Pembrokeshire or north-east Wales, the arms manufacturer, horse dealer, surgeon or sexton. But even the most trivial act of violence in the quietest village or parish, neglected by almost all our sources, must have had a profound impact upon all who witnessed it. Over fifty years after it occurred, Richard Gough still vividly recalled the one 'skirmage' which took place in Myddle during the war. An eight-man royalist foraging party from Shrawardine was attacked and scattered by eight parliamentarians out of Morton Corbett. Two royalists were captured and subsequently hanged. The royalist commander, Cornet Collins, was 'shot through the body with a carbine shot' and carried to a house he had recently plundered. 'Mr Rodericke was sent for to pray with him. I went with him, and saw the cornet lying on the bed, and much blood running along the floor'. He died the following day.

Memories

When he wrote this account in the opening years of the eighteenth century, Gough could draw on first-hand experience of the war years — he was born in the 1630s and clearly witnessed most of the events he described. But by then the civil war was quickly slipping into mere history as death carried off the participants. Of the senior officers who had fought in Wales, very few survived to see the Glorious Revolution of 1688, and none appears to have outlived the century. Sir Roger Mostyn died in 1690, Charles Gerard, earl of Macclesfield, in 1694, and Roger Whitley, the civil war governor of Aberystwyth, in 1697. Yet for many generations thereafter the civil war lived on in stories, traditions and legends, their tones so fresh and colourful that the authors might

Despite the dislocation of the civil war, the post-war years saw considerable building activity. During the 1650s, a number of grand houses were erected in England, several of them reflecting a fashion for a more compact style, for all the rooms to be gathered into a single block rather than arranged in several wings. Although far fewer buildings appear to have been erected in Wales in the post-war period, there are signs of activity, particularly in the north-east. Henblas, Llanasa (top), built in 1645, and Trimley Hall, Llanfynydd (bottom), built around 1653, both reflect this more compact centralized architectural style (Photograph — National Monuments Record, Wales, by courtesy of Thomas Lloyd).

even have witnessed the events. Visitors to Wales in the eighteenth and nineteenth century heard and recorded a rich, vibrant corpus of folklore connected with the civil war. The huge population movements of the late ninteenth century and the rediscovery of 'professional' history, with its emphasis upon contemporary written evidence and its suspicion of tales and tradition, did much to undermine this and to shatter the remaining links between the civil war era and our own times.

Francis Kilvert, the rector of Clyro and diarist of southern Radnorshire in the 1870s, heard and noted down a rich crop of civil war stories related by his parishoners. One told of Charles I passing through the area during the civil war. The story may be accurate, for Charles did march through on 6 August 1645, shortly after his uncomfortable meeting with the Peaceable Army. It was almost his last visit to Wales.

Castle House, Monmouth, stands on the site of part of the demolished castle. Following the war and the destruction of Raglan, the Somerset family, marquises of Worcester, needed a new seat in the county. They built Castle House in the 1670s, a modest but well appointed town house, complete with ornate plastered ceilings and fine internal woodwork.

> *While talking to Davies outside I heard old William Pritchard within coughing violently. I went in and sat some time talking to him and his niece Mrs Evans... I asked him if he had ever heard any talk of Charles I ever having been about in this country. 'Oh yes', he said, 'I have a jug that the King once drunk out of at Blaen cerdi. He had breakfast that day in Brecon, dined at Gwernyfed and slept at Harpton, passing through Newchurch. His army was with him and riding two and two in the narrow lanes[;] the line reached from Pen Vaen in Newchurch, through the village up to Blaen cerdi. At Blaen cerdi all the farm people, boys and girls ran out to see the King pass. The King was afoot. He stopped opposite the house and asked my ancestress Mary Bayliss to give him something to drink. She went to the house and fetched him milk and water in this jug... and at the same time a chair from the house, which she placed in the fold, that the King might sit down and rest while drinking the milk'.*

Tredegar House was massively extended by Sir William Morgan around 1670, and is probably the finest restoration period mansion in Wales. The old medieval house, in which Charles I had briefly lodged in 1645, became a rear wing of the new mansion. Arranged around a central court, the new wings were of red brick, symmetrically designed and with slightly projecting corners.

In March 1870 the memory of the king's passing visit on a hot summer's day towards the end of the war remained clear and fresh. An event which must have been over in a few minutes lived on ten generations or more after it occurred. In this, as much as all the ruined castles and soliders' graves, we have a true measure of the impact of civil war in Wales.

Index

Reference to photographs and illustrations appear in italic script